The Zombie Memes of Dixie

THE ZOMBIE MEMES
OF DIXIE

SCOTT ROMINE

Mercer University Lamar Memorial Lectures No. 60

THE UNIVERSITY OF GEORGIA PRESS   Athens

© 2024 by the University of Georgia Press
Athens, Georgia 30602
www.ugapress.org
All rights reserved
Designed by Rebecca A. Norton
Set in 10/14 Sabon LT Pro

Most University of Georgia Press titles are
available from popular e-book vendors.

Printed digitally

Library of Congress Cataloging-in-Publication Data
Names: Romine, Scott, author.
Title: The zombie memes of Dixie / Scott Romine,
University of North Carolina at Greensboro.
Other titles: Mercer University Lamar memorial lectures ; no. 60.
Description: Athens : University of Georgia Press, [2024] |
Series: Mercer University Lamar Memorial Lectures ; No. 60 |
Includes bibliographical references and index.
Identifiers: LCCN 2024023265 | ISBN 9780820367767 (hardback) |
ISBN 9780820367774 (paperback) | ISBN 9780820367781 (epub) |
ISBN 9780820367798 (pdf)
Subjects: LCSH: Social groups—Southern States. | Memes—Southern
States. | Slavery—Social aspects—Southern States. |
Southern States—Social life and customs—Public opinion. |
Southern States—In popular culture.
Classification: LCC F209.R664 2024 |
DDC 975/.0049607—dc23/eng/20240718
LC record available at https://lccn.loc.gov/2024023265

Contents

Illustrations

Foreword

In October 2022, Scott Romine gave the Eugenia Dorothy Blount Lamar Memorial Lectures at Mercer University. Not one to shy away from asking difficult questions—is there really a South?—Romine chose as his topic the category of meme to show how Dixie continues to be invoked in attempts to explain "the South." He posits that the best new southern studies could do to try to move beyond the Confederate nationalist impulse in twentieth-century lost cause redemptive narratives was put scare quotes around the term "the South" to signify that it was not the old southern studies. While the idea of many Souths might be a better way to approach the region, Romine deploys the category of meme to show how pithy images and words function as code for an idea of a South in the decades leading up to the American Civil War. The zombie trope helps us see that this imagery remains entrenched in descriptions of the American South. Hospitality is the way people who inhabit the region are described, even as violence is a daily occurrence. "Bless her heart" does a lot of work that southerners understand, even if outsiders are bemused by it. These lectures are at odds with the intent of the Lamar Lectures because they challenge the very notion that there is a South to describe at all. But they reveal a truth about the bequest that established them: almost all attempts to explain the South have to deal with the formation of the Confederate States of America and then the work done by those to redeem the ideas of that particular past in the absence of a separate nation whose trappings they could appeal to.

In the mid-1950s, Eugenia Dorothy Blount Lamar made the bequest to Mercer University, located in her hometown of Macon, Georgia, "to provide lectures of the very highest scholarship which will aid in the permanent preservation of the values of Southern culture, history, and literature." Until the late 1980s, scholars hewed closely to Lamar's implicit understanding of southern culture as white and decidedly upper class, but since the 1990s, they have been asking questions about enslaved people, landless people, and the lack of widespread civil rights in the region. In the past decade, the critiques of those values have become more pointed. But Romine's lectures ask us to consider whether attempts to move beyond Lamar's understanding of those values are even possible. Whether the thesis and evidence are agreeable to the reader, his lectures show how potent the attraction of the South remains for many in the region and beyond.

Mercer University earned a National Endowment of the Humanities Challenge Grant in 2014 that over the course of five years yielded a $2 million endowment that underwrites extensive programming around southern studies at the university, including the Lamar Memorial Lecture Series. In 2017, Mercer established the Spencer B. King Jr. Center for Southern Studies to house both the endowment and southern studies programming. Named after a longtime history department faculty member, the center fosters critical discussions about the many meanings of the South. The center is the only such entity dedicated to the education and enrichment solely of undergraduate students, and its primary purpose is to examine the region's complex history and culture through courses, conversations, and events that are open, honest, and accessible.

The committee would like to thank in particular two people who helped pull off the lectures and the manuscript publication. Our program coordinator William Aultman helped bring these lectures to Mercer and Macon by facilitating travel and reservations, while Beth Snead has been a helpful guide for the series at the University of Georgia Press. To listen to the lectures is simple compared to shepherding them into publication.

We hope that these lectures encourage more conversation about what it means to think about the American South.

Douglas E. Thompson, Chair

LAMAR MEMORIAL LECTURE COMMITTEE

DIRECTOR, SPENCER B. KING JR.,

CENTER FOR SOUTHERN STUDIES

Acknowledgments

I was delighted to receive an invitation to deliver the 2020 Lamar Lectures at Mercer University. Many thanks to David Davis, Sarah Gardner, and Douglas Thompson for their hospitality during my visit, which took place at the height of the COVID pandemic. Despite being perhaps the first Lamar Lecturer to speak through a mask, I was honored to join a list of scholars that includes two members of my dissertation committee, Fred Hobson and John Shelton Reed. I found to be true what Hobson says in his preface to his *The Southern Writer in the Postmodern World*: the Lamar Lectures offer scholars the rare to "undertake a subject about which he or she has *something* to say, would like venture certain opinions on," but without the imperative of "pronouncing the final word." In my case, the meant the opportunity to consider a question that I likely would not have taken up in a monograph: namely, what *kind* of thing are the things southerners say define them?

Many thanks also to the University of Georgia Press and especially for their patience while I completed the manuscript. A heavy administrative load, a pandemic, and various other distractions made this a longer process than desirable, but Beth Snead was both understanding and helpful as the project progressed. Thanks also to MJ Devaney for her careful copyediting, which strengthened the manuscript.

I have long been gratified to have such excellent colleagues both at UNCG and in the field of southern studies. A conference at Mercer hosted by the Southern Intellectual History Circle and another on "What Was the New Southern Studies?" offered opportunities to present early versions of some of the ideas offered here. My respondents at SIHC, Bryan Giemza and Monica Miller, and others at the conference—notably, Sarah Gardner and Steven Stowe—offered valuable feedback, as did Leigh Anne Duck, Katherine Henninger, Erich Nunn, and others at the later conference. Thanks also to my daughters, Olivia and Isabella, and my wife, Karen Weyler, for chatting over some of the questions raised here, although none of them, I should add, seem to be persuaded by my answers. Special thanks to Jon Smith for various zoom meetings, conference discussions, and written rejoinders to my work that have, over the years, sharpened my thinking about the South.

The Zombie Memes of Dixie

A South Made of Memes

It is a truth universally acknowledged that no thing said twice about the South ever stops being said. This is sometimes true even when the thing isn't said about the South in the first place: witness William Faulkner on the past being neither dead nor past. A few years ago, I was asked to serve as the contrarian member of a panel debating the existence of southern visual art. I know nothing about the topic, and I was asked to step in because the previously scheduled contrarian—the head of the art department—was unable to attend. But on expressing doubt that there was a coherent thing called southern art (because I doubt there is a coherent thing called the South), I soon found myself on recognizable ground. There certainly was such a thing, I was told, and one of its principal characteristics was that it displayed a distinctive "sense of place."

Sense of place! That phrase, "so hackneyed," as John Shelton Reed observes, that "it is a cliché to call it a cliché," was trotted out as empirical evidence, solid as a stone, proving that southern art could be confused with no other.[1] My fellow panelists—and most of the audience, I think—were shocked when I voiced skepticism about a distinctively southern "sense of place." Hadn't I read Eudora Welty's "Place in Fiction?" I had, and while the essay references Faulkner, it also references Gustave Flaubert, Emily Brontë, Anton Chekhov,

Katherine Mansfield, James Joyce, Ernest Hemingway, Jane Austen, Thomas Hardy, Ivan Turgenev, and "the authors of the books of the Old Testament"; it does not include the term "sense of place," nor the words "South" or "southern"; it doubts the very existence of "regional writing."[2] Two panelists, both self-identified southerners, offered vivid accounts of their personal southern senses of place. These, I responded, were very different accounts of very different places. What was this "South" binding them? One panelist was from Florida; were we sure that it was even *in* the South? (It was OK: she was from northern Florida—the southern part.) Why was it necessary to represent their disparate accounts as *southern*? Because both states had joined the Confederacy? Were they certain that no one in Costa Rica—or, for that matter, Ohio—had similar attachments to place?

I begin with the anecdote because it marks a professional failure. According to no less an authority than Wikipedia, I am the "they" said to "argue that the U.S. South has always been a construct."[3] Although not necessarily reflecting my own views, this is a fair, if overly generalized, perspective shared by a number of scholars who in the 1990s began to question the romantic assumptions governing the discipline of southern literary studies. The field of southern literature up until this time seemed belatedly yoked to what amounted to a blood-and-soil, *volkgeist*-haunted conception of literary history—the idea, as William Gilmore Simms puts it, that "to write *from* a people is to *write* a people—to make them live—to endow them with a life and name—to preserve them with a history forever."[4] Literature, on this view, came from the ground up, as Alexander Beaufort Meek explains in his 1857 *Songs and Poems of the South*: "The Poetry of a country should be a faithful expression of its physical and moral characteristics. . . . [Its] sentiments [should] be such as naturally arise under the influence of its climate, its institutions, habits of life, and social condition. Verse, so fashioned and colored, is as much the genuine product and growth of a Land, as its trees or flowers. It partakes of the raciness of the soil."[5]

As a disciplinary matter, a number of embarrassments had to be explained away. The southern people had a surfeit of history, so much as to amount to a *burden*, but, for much of the region's history, they did not have much literature to show for it. The problem was illustrated by an anecdote, probably fictitious but illustrative nonetheless, of an 1856 resolution that "there be a Southern literature" and that Simms "be requested to write the literature."[6] This made sense, because, according to the romantic nationalism of the nineteenth century, literature expressed the distinctive qualities of the nation. If, according to Johann Gottfried Herder's famous dictum, poets are the creators of the nation around them, it followed that a South aspiring to nationhood ought to have poets. It ought to have books, *De Bow's* observes in 1858, books that reflected "Southern thought, Southern feeling, Southern manners, customs, and peculiarities." *De Bow's* does note an emerging literature "more 'racy of the soil' than formerly"—perhaps the editors knew Meek's volume, but the magazine acknowledges that the South still lagged.[7] A similar conclusion was reached after the war by J. B. Wardlaw, who asks why the "old ante-bellum life . . . did not produce a literature of its own." With "our southern national feeling as a thought-soil"—feeling amounting to the intensity of an "ethnic passion"—why had no southerner done for the South what "Sir Walter, a Scotchman, did for Scotland?"[8]

In retrospect, the scholarly explanation for the deficit, offered first by Allen Tate and receiving its fullest expression in the work of Lewis P. Simpson, was what Simpson describes as an "alienation from alienation" experienced by the "Southern literary mind," which "did not undergo an experience of alienation from its own—the Southern—society."[9] As Louis Rubin argues, "The South did not produce many great writers before 1920 because it did not detach its artists sufficiently from community life," the "nature and hold of the Southern community" having provided "a sufficiently complex emotional, intellectual, and aesthetic order to accommodate all its members."[10] On this view, the South was too organic to have grown a literature.

But even though southern writers eventually managed to alienate themselves to an extent, Rubin's generation still understood the canon of southern literature much as it had been understood a century earlier: as expressing the essence of a singular, distinctive southern people. Drawing on the romantic idea of the soil from the nineteenth century, Donald Davidson explains that the "indigenous materials" of literature "will derive some of their shape and force from the *genius loci*—the region itself," just as "regions will develop their arts as they develop their people and ways of life," a relationship he describes elsewhere as the "autochthonous ideal."[11] Southern literature was different because the South was different; it came from the ground up. In this way, "sense of place" could rise organically from the *genius loci*. Thus Frederick J. Hoffman, in a 1961 essay, grounds "sense of place" in things like "the Southern character," "Southern tradition," "the Southerner" (assumed to be white), "the Southern mind," "the Southerner's love of place," place's "specific Southern quality," and the "atmospheric quality of the Southern place" (of which heat is said to be "always present, even if momentarily it may not exist").[12] The idea that heat is "always present" seems to suggest that the South is hot even when it is cold, a dubious proposition considered as a mere matter of meteorology. And yet the claim has the ring of truth. Some years ago at the North Carolina zoo, I overheard a mother say to her complaining child, "What can I tell you? It's July in the South, it's going to be hot." On a different day, she could not have substituted "January" and "cold." The South, as we all know, isn't cold; it's hot, and not just hot, but . . . well, you probably know that it's humid, too.

To a cohort of scholars weaned on a hermeneutics of suspicion, this singular South said to underwrite southern writing appeared increasingly questionable, as did its constitutive parts. What, precisely, was this "Southern character"? Was there but one? Did the southern community truly accommodate all its members? For many scholars associated with the new southern studies, the South met what Ian Hacking identifies as the core criteria of a construction, namely, that an X is "not determined by the nature of things; it is not inevitable," even though "in the present state of affairs, X is taken for granted; X appears to be inevitable."[13] Taking the South for granted seemed itself an act of will. As Jon Smith has suggested, for many of us, constructivist assumptions derived not so much from "some eruption of reality-defying philosophical idealism or of rampant postmodernity" but rather from growing up in a South that didn't seem that distinctive.[14] I grew up, for example, in a generic subdivision in metro Atlanta that, despite being outside the I-285 perimeter ("Atlanta's Mason-Dixon line"), looked and sounded little like the South I saw on television. In addition, constructivism appeared to offer a reasonable return on the investment of academic labor. Demand seemed low for yet another essay locating the sense of place in this or that novel from the southern canon or for one taking another lap around the critical loop described by Michael Kreyling: "There was a South in history, there is one today, and this South, this 'entity,' engenders a literature which then reflexively identifies and certifies it."[15] Lastly, constructivism enabled a kind of interventionist criticism since, as Hacking observes, it is typically "critical of the status quo" and often assumes that "we would be much better off if X were done away with, or at least radically transformed."[16]

The short version of a more complicated history is that the new southern studies has had moderate success in placing scare quotes around terms like "sense of place." Patricia Yaeger, in fact, singles out "a peculiarly southern sense of place" as one of the "mystifications" constituting the Dixie Limited of southern literature whose rails she was aiming to dynamite when she published *Dirt and Desire* in 2000.[17] So far as literary studies are concerned, the rails are pretty well dynamited by now. Today, it's rare to encounter the *volkgeist*-haunted assumptions of what Jennifer Rae Greeson calls the "one-people-one-poetry pseudonationalist model of 'southern literature,'" the poetry and the people arising in harmonious concert from the southern soil.[18] To a significant degree, we do, as Leigh Anne Duck puts it, "Southern studies without 'the South,'" so much so that it is now possible to imagine a cold day in both southern writing and southern history.[19]

But it's impossible to find a cold variant of the internet meme proclaiming that "down here in the South, it's not the heat—it's the humidity!" Like the appeal to a "sense of place" during my failed stint as an art critic, the insistence on the South's being "hot, and humid too" speaks to more than a mere trickle-down failure of academic discourses. At least in my case, it reveals a rather profound inability to predict the future. True, I note in a 2002 essay that "for over a century, reports of the South's demise have been greatly exaggerated," but when I wrote that sentence, I wouldn't have thought an academic conversation was necessary to disrupt perceptions of a coherent southern identity or—to introduce the term that most often aggregates the South today—*culture*.[20] Entropy and standardization, I thought, would do the trick. In 2003, when Larry J. Griffin and Ashley B. Thompson defined "symbolic southernness" as "largely ancestral, honorific, and selectively enacted rather than rooted in the routines of daily life or the attributions of nonSoutherners" and found not only that the South was disappearing (and that it had been disappearing for a while) but also that the *southerner* was disappearing, I wouldn't have thought that in 2017, I would witness the publication of a book like Christopher A. Cooper and H. Gibbs Knotts's *The Resilience of Southern Identity* in which the resilience in question consists largely of southerners saying the same old things about the South.[21] As constructions go, the South has proven more durable than I expected. To say that gender is a construction is axiomatic; to say the same of the South is still to invite raised eyebrows. Of course, in 2003, I also hadn't heard of Facebook, Twitter, or memes, which have, in the interim, revealed a great deal about how sociality is mediated and always has been.

The question I wish to explore, briefly stated, is how and

why a set of ideas and associations mostly originating over a few decades prior to 1861 in an explicitly ethnonationalist defense of a slave-based economy have mutated in a way allowing them to survive and even flourish in a multiracial, multiethnic region characterized by mobility, flexible labor, and exponentially expanding bandwidth. Transported forward in time, a southerner from the year 1850 would find today's Southeast incomprehensible, but if we started talking about the South, much of what we'd say would sound familiar. By zombie memes of Dixie, I mean those propositions, types, beliefs, associations, clichés, tropes—ideas in the broadest and, I wish to stress this, *vaguest* sense of that term—that simply won't die. Often saturated with affect, their curious relation to the material world is suggested by words like "stereotype" and "impression" that originated as printing terms, but quickly extended into figurative meanings. ("Impression" is further helpful in signaling an idea or feeling formed without careful thought or on the basis of scant evidence.) And yet for all their slipperiness, they remain stubbornly stuck to something called the South. My subject matter is familiar, which is not surprising because familiarity is essential to the concept of memes. On the one (romantic) hand, there is a South of hospitality, tradition, leisure, localism, chivalry, feudalism, rootedness, paternalism, thick social bonds, and anticapitalism (or antiwhatever the "modern" economy is called at the time); on the (abject) other, there is a South of violence, squalor, backwardness, racism, poverty, and provincialism. You probably know what these look like; if I were to ask you to think (or tell me) about "the South," ideas and images would quickly come to mind, and the ones that did would likely reveal whether you're a southerner or not.

I'm interested in how those ideas and associations got in our minds and what they're doing there—how they constitute what Jennifer Rae Greeson calls "this South that we hold collectively in our minds." In simplest terms, my subject is not the mind of the South but the South of the mind or, less elegantly, the South in the brain. I share with Greeson the belief that this South "is not—could not possibly be—a fixed real place," although believing it to be so often acts a crucial precondition for what, I argue, the South actually does: assemble people into groups, sometimes even into "a people."[22] Here, I follow Bruno Latour in preferring "group" to alternative terms—race, people, nation, culture, civilization, society, community—precisely because in those terms are embedded assumptions (or arguments) about what the group is (or should be).[23] I proceed, then, on the premise that the South is best understood not as a representation of the Southeast (the "real place") but of southerners assembling under the banner of southernness. In terms of physics, I treat the South as wave, not particle; in terms of grammar, as verb, not noun.

Approaching the South as something other than a fixed entity will entail a hermeneutics of credulity that asks why things like a "southern sense of place" and "the south is hot and humid too" continue to be replicated—much more successfully, in fact, than "the South is a construct." As an empirical claim, "the south is hot and humid too" is falsifiable and sometimes false, as is the case as I write on a cool, dry May afternoon in North Carolina. As it turns out, if one adds heat (in degrees Fahrenheit) to humidity (as percentage), North Carolina during the month of July is slightly less southern than Illinois. But the claim is not primarily empirical in nature, as is suggested by the Quora responses to the question of "how do people in the American South deal with the extreme heat and humidity in the summer?" clearly posed by an outsider:

> It's just part of being a Southerner. We sit out on our *verandahs*, sip mint julips and fan ourselves complainin' 'bout this awful heat and the *weatha*.
>
> . . .
>
> I've always believed the oppressive heat here is why we talk slowly here, too. I know it is for me.
>
> . . .
>
> I think I can speak for my region when I say, "A least we're not havin' to deal with those snowplows and bulky coats. I'll take a wrinkled, damp sundress with flip flops, a frizzy ponytail and big glass of sweet tea anyday.

Bless y'all's hearts!

. . .

> Basically, we just make do. We complain to the stranger be-
> hind us in line at the grocery store. We always say, "It's not the
> heat, it's the humidity!"—and though it's become a cliche at
> this point, it's absolutely true.[24]

Many of the hundred plus responses offer an insider's perspective, whether by their lapsing into orthographical dialect ("*weatha*," "havin'"), restating and inverting an implicit antagonism ("better a damp sundress than your Yankee
snowplows"), connecting the heat to other markers of group
identity (mint juleps, slow speech, sweet tea), or explicitly
speaking for the region. Heat and humidity have something
to do with the weather, but more to do with delineating an
inside and an outside. This is why, for Hoffman, the heat is
"always present"; it must be, if "the Southern character" is
to survive a cold snap. Pointing to the weather, these southerners have (as the saying goes) three fingers pointing back at
themselves, a rule of thumb that, as we'll see, has been true of
southerners for more than two centuries.

A strong predictor, I argue, of a meme's fecundity—its capacity to replicate—is its capacity to "anchor" a group identity. My emphasis on memes as *group-forming* replicators has
the effect of slightly but significantly altering how Richard
Dawkins defines them in *The Selfish Gene*. There, he characterizes memes as the cultural equivalent of genes: the basic
"unit of cultural transmission" or replication. His definition
of "unit" is ambiguous: God is a unit; an architectural style
is a unit; "Darwin's theory" is a unit, although, he adds, only
that part of the theory "held in common by all brains that understand the theory." Delineating that portion would prove
difficult enough with Darwin, to say nothing of God. More
significantly, he provides no working definition of "culture,"
which at times gravitates toward an Arnoldian conception of
high culture (he asserts that Beethoven's ninth, even a "single
phrase" of it, is a meme) and at other times toward a crude
ontological idea of a "soup of human culture" consisting of
anything this side of the culture/nature divide.[25]

That Dawkins is not able to offer a clear definition of culture is unsurprising; it's a notoriously muddy concept used in a variety of contradictory ways. More unexpected is that he avoids an obvious, although imperfect, analogy: as genes are to species, memes are to groups. The reason, I suspect, is that God, or the "religious meme complex," operates for Dawkins as a kind of ur-meme, orienting in particular his argument that "a cultural trait may have evolved in the way that it has, simply because it is *advantageous to itself*."[26] Just a virus need not serve any function to its host, he argues, so memes need only worm their way into brains in order to replicate. That the "god delusion" (to borrow the title of another of his books) drives his analysis is suggested by the "true ambition" he mentions in his notes on the chapter. "I want," he writes, "to claim an almost limitless power for slightly inaccurate self-replicating entities"—that is, to explain the persistence of *error* within the "milieu of human culture."[27] But, as Jonathan Haidt argues, delusion may be beneficial because it facilitates social cohesion. Following Durkheim, Haidt describes religion as a "team sport" dependent not merely on a set belief about God but on the experience of belonging to a group holding those beliefs.[28] Agnosticism generates no parallel group formation.

On the one hand, I have attempted to follow Dawkins in being skeptical of memes as reliable descriptors of reality. Although the one Quora respondent insists that "heat and humidity" is both a "cliché" and "absolutely true," it seems wise to resist the conclusion of the character in Josephine Humphreys's *Rich in Love* who pays attention to clichés *because* they are true.[29] "Otherwise," she explains, "they wouldn't have achieved cliché status."[30] That correspondence to reality does not predict replication is an easy conclusion to reach in an age of clicks, likes, and retweets, when the Enlightenment seems not so much an unfinished project, to borrow Jürgen Habermas's phrase, as an abandoned one. More predictive, I suggest, is the capacity of memes to assemble groups that will, in turn, replicate the meme.[31] Here it may be worth noting

that there is a Flat Earth Society, but no round earth equivalent; mere facticity, in other words, may impede the formation of inside and outside.

A neutral descriptive account of evolution "held in common by all brains that understand the theory" is thus not,
for my purposes, a meme until it creates sides—a bumper
sticker, say, displaying that you're on Team Darwin (a Christian ichthys with legs, accompanied by "Darwin" or "I'm
with Darwin") or on Team Christian (a Christian ichthys
marked "Truth" eating the legged Darwinian ichthys). As a
historical matter, Darwin has replicated pretty effectively to
tell us which side we're on—for southerners, usually the anti-
Darwin side. In the context of the Scopes Monkey Trial of
1925, the Darwin meme might signal an invading enemy bent
on destroying "religion" with "science" or occasion countermemes, such as Billy Rose's hit song "You Can't Make a
Monkey out of Me," which, in correcting a claim Darwin
didn't make, still offers an effective retort to the other side. It
might catalyze particular projects of southern self-fashioning
such as the one offered in the 1930 Agrarian manifesto *I'll
Take My Stand*. But it could conceivably be enlisted on behalf
of Team South in, for example, a deployment of his theory
of racial difference in support of white supremacist constructions of the South.

Memes reproduce, according to Dawkins, by renting space
our brains and doing so "at the expense of rival memes."[32]
I've noted that no thing said twice about the South ever stops
being said, but of course it isn't true. If "sense of place" has
achieved cliché status, it has done so by competing successfully against thousands of proto-clichés that never made it.
There are two methodological difficulties here. The first is the
potential pointlessness of the exercise. As an analytical unit,
the meme has little to recommend it. What is there, after all,
to be said about a cliché or—to use other derogatory terms
associated with what I'm calling memes—a commonplace, a
stereotype, or a talking point? Quite a lot, actually, if we consider thick contextual analyses such as Anthony Szczesiul's

The Southern Hospitality Myth or M. M. Manring's *Slave in a Box: The Strange Career of Aunt Jemima.* I came across Manring's book in 2018, during the early stages of this project, after I began looking into why there were still millions of copies of this image in supermarkets nationwide. Why did it continue to replicate long after the "mammy" been properly banished from public view? Manring's book addressed my question by showing how this "weird sort of Confederate memorial" had mutated over time to represent Black servility in a range of historically specific moments.[33]

My approach, however, differs substantially from Szczesiul's and Manring's in attending to memes in their most conceptually impoverished and therefore most easily replicated form, namely, as they appear in a phrase or image, or adorning a T-shirt or bumper sticker. To the criticism that, reduced to meme form, the South is scarcely worth talking about, I'd respond that it's the South we talk about most of the time and always have. Rather than focusing, then, as an intellectual historian might, on the best that has been thought and said about the South, I focus on what's been thought and said the most: the genetically simplified, *viral* forms that replicate most easily. Moreover, I'm interested in the constitutive superficiality of memes, their capacity to represent dense "social," "historical," or "cultural" data in highly compressed form. The group meaning of "Robert E. Lee" or "Sherman," for example, requires no deep knowledge of either. Probably it is damaged by such knowledge—that Lee blundered here or that Sherman showed mercy there.[34] In a similar way, "Faulkner" can be said to *belong* to southerners who have never read him and in a way impossible for a Faulkner scholar born in Detroit.[35] I've found it useful to think of memes as floating bits of Styrofoam giving the impression of icebergs. Many brains hosting the Sherman meme could not produce the general's full name, and more than one student has professed to me the importance of the Civil War to southern identity (including their own) without being able to identify what century the war was fought in. The synecdochical power of memes—their capacity to evoke some larger, formless "whole"—is significant, for surely the Civil War *is* important to many southerners, however little (or much) they know about it. It affects the way they assemble as southerners—mostly, I suspect, through an intuitive identification with the losing side. As a (mere) proposition, "The South lost the Civil War" is arguable on a number of fronts: many people in the South (enslaved people, Unionists) "won" the war, and few would argue today that a triumphant Confederacy, as a slaveholding republic independent of the United States, would have benefited in the long run. But such arguments are weak against the power of assembly generated by "the experience of defeat," as C. Vann Woodward memorializes the loss. And this is true however attenuated an individual's relationship is to that "experience." "Experience," like "memory," is word that evokes something different from what it means. Especially when we hear of *collective* experiences, *collective* memories, or *collective* childhoods, we can be sure that we are in the presence of memes.

A second methodological difficulty is explaining how, precisely, memes rent space in your brain. What psychological wage does it pay? What gives one an advantage over another? I confess to a disadvantage here, since, to the best of my knowledge, my brain is relatively impervious to Dixie memes. Growing up, I viewed Confederate soldiers as menacing figures (the sinister gray uniforms!) fighting against the flag that adorned the uniform of Sugar Ray Leonard at the 1976 Olympics. As a Cold War kid for whom the bicentennial marked an important childhood moment—dressed as Uncle Sam, I emceed our third-grade celebration of Great Americans, none of whom, as I recall, were Confederates—I lacked any sense that my side had lost the Civil War. The enemies of my imagined community were redcoats and red Soviets, not Yankees. I can't recall a single childhood friend who had been born in Gwinnett County, while many had moved from places like New York, California, the Philippines, Illinois, Cuba, and Puerto Rico. None of us had "roots" in the place. If pressed, I would guess that the autochthonous domain of Lilburn, Georgia, was very similar to its analogue in metropolitan Cleveland. In any event, little in my childhood taught me that I lived in the South, belonged to it, or was classified as a kind of person defined by it. This, along with a gradually acquired sense that being seen as a southerner entailed certain minor costs, likely explains my intuitive skepticism of, for example, the idea that southerners possess a special or distinctive "sense of place." The South names a group with which my affiliation is weak, at best—perhaps on a level with "Georgian" or "North Carolinian." For this reason, the ties that bind southerners often appear to me as, to borrow Kwame Anthony Appiah's phrase, the lies that bind.

But to view memes this way is questionable on two fronts. First, they're not lies, if we understand lies as intentional misrepresentations of the truth. Whatever might be said about the argument that the Civil War wasn't about slavery, people making the argument believe, passionately, that it's true. That they do is essential to the meme's functionality. Second, cool skepticism toward memes potentially shorts their psychological and social compensations. *Southernness*, to adapt Haidt's argument, is a team sport, and for better or for worse, "the experience of defeat" has proven affectively and socially sticky. It has caused southerners to think of themselves as southerners and more importantly to *feel* themselves to be so. In order to do so, or because it does so, it generates copies. Every Confederate monument, every "South Will Rise Again" bumper sticker, every rebel flag represents a variant of the idea, which is often accompanied by the notion that the experience of defeat can be reversed. But it hardly follows that the groups assembled by the meme are mechanical reproductions of one another. For Woodward, the "experience of defeat" constructed the South as a check on American triumphalism and imperialism. In a recent piece titled "The Troubled Task of Defining Southern Literature in 2021," Ed Tarkington attempts to progressively repurpose the meme. Declaring that the "real war never ended" (because white supremacy never ended), he, like Quentin Compson before him, concludes by not hating the South and by declaring his desire "to lose the war—again, and again, and again, until it's really, finally over."[36] What this means is less than clear, but Tarkington is obviously trying to form a group different from the "South Will Rise Again" crowd, who want to "win" the war, albeit in a similarly vague way. Both groups, however, exclude groups who didn't lose the war, including millions of immigrants to the South who may or may not identify as southerners and the large majority of Black people who do. That these groups share a claim on *the South* with neo-Confederates suggests, simply, that the South so-called is less self-evident than many suppose.

Even so, it requires no great prophetic skill to foresee that the South will continue to have lost the war—again, and again, and again—and that having done so will continue to assemble the South. Whatever argument might be made that the "the South won the war," it's important to observe that an argument is required. Consider the apparent novelty of Heather Cox Richardson's *How the South Won the Civil War* (2020), which is a variant of Albion Tourgée's 1888 claim that "the South surrendered at Appomattox, and the North has been surrendering ever since," which is a variant of Edward Pollard's 1868 claim that "the true cause fought for in the late war has not been 'lost' immeasurably or irrevocably, but is yet in a position to be 'regained' by the South," all the Souths in question boiling down to projects of white supremacy.[37] Conversely, "the South lost the war" needs no argument; it seems intuitively true.

Successful memes resist falsification, which isn't to say that they require proof. Often they constitute "folk knowledge" as defined by Adolph Reed: "what we know because we know it."[38] But not only are memes self-evident, they act as self-evidence, facilitating our assembly *as us*. As Immanuel Wallerstein observes, conceptions of culture are *typically* based on presumed group values for which "we have in practice virtually zero hard evidence."[39] How, indeed, would one go about proving a distinctively southern "sense of place"? What empirical data might distinguish southern hospitality from Minnesota nice? "What," Donald Nonini poses in a devious question, "are the [cultural] traits that genuine southerners claim to have and that non-southerners lack but might acquire and thereby change their identities to become southerners?"[40] It's devious because, for one thing, it assumes that a genuine southern identity can, like some religious identities (but not others), be *acquired*—that it's not, to cite another Faulknerian meme, a matter of being "born there." For another, any trait claimed by genuine southerners—showing hospitality, having good manners, appreciating sweet tea—correlates imperfectly, if at all, with those who consider themselves genuine southerners. At the same time, if there is no test of southernness, there can be no southerners, only people living in the Southeast. The philosopher Antony Flew coined the phrase "no true Scotsman" to describe a logical fallacy "commonly associated with protecting a preferred group"—thus, the Scotsman who commits a heinous crime is "no true Scotsman"—but without a condition of belonging, a line separating true southerners from the other kind, there can be no group, only an address.[41] And if, empirically, the line boils down to "zero hard evidence" or a statistical variation, it must be observed that no one belongs to a statistical variation.

An Entity Made of Memes

In George Washington Cable's *John March, Southerner* (1894), a character named Barbara Garnet asks the title character, her husband-to-be, an intriguing question: "What is it in the South we Southerners love so?" The reason she is asks is that when a visiting Yankee had posed the question to her, she had fumblingly "intimated that it was simply something a North-ern-er can't un-der-stand." (In other words, you'd have to be born there.) The answer she and March come up with is that "it" is a "sort o' something," a "certain ungeographical South-within-the-South—as portable and intangible as—as—the souls in our bodies." So far as I'm concerned, that's a good answer, and they should have stopped there. But of course they don't. Barbara isn't quite sure *what* she loves, but she knows that, because she's a southerner, she loves it. And because she loves it, it must be "in the South"; some *thing* in Dixie must make it like no other land "all the wide world over."[42] In one way, I think Cable has the scene slightly wrong. I've generally found that "what is the South?" is a hard question that often ends up producing a vague "sort o' something" sort of response. By contrast, "what makes the South the South?"—a variant of Barbara's initial inquiry—is much easier, reliably generating the "grounded differences" orienting this project. But while these differences are evoked as characteristic of the South (as the basis of identitarian investiture), I want to resist the conclusion that they're characteristic of the Southeast (the geographical region). If your ear does not readily accept such phrases as "southeastern belle," "southeastern hospitality," or "southeastern way of life," it's because the South and the Southeast are different. To overstate the case, the South is no more a guide to the Southeast than an urban legend is a guide to a city. It is, however, an excellent guide to assembling southerners.

The idea of an ungrounded South often shatters against quasi-commonsensical arguments wherein the South is shown, after all, to come "from the ground up." In his 1972 *Enduring South*, for example, John Shelton Reed concedes that "like race, and religion in its noncreedal aspects, region is a summary construct." But unlike race or religion, he argues, it possesses an "*intrinsic* aspect" based, in part, on the "simple fact" that "residence in a particular area, implying exposure to a particular climate, soil, and terrain, will produce distinctive effects."[43] In other words, the South makes southerners, not, as I suggest, the other way around. In a more complex reversion to geography, C. Hugh Holman argues that "there is no real 'South'" except as a "high level abstraction" within which "land, language, race, climate, mountain and plain, pine and palm are mixed together in a common conception." While for Reed geography exists in a causal relation to the "summary construct," for Holman the notional South *includes* geographical features—or rather conceptions of them—and is shored up by stipulated traits ("a homogeneity of belief," a "dream of a traditional social order," an "obsession . . . with the past"). But since even that South seems shaky, Holman goes on to argue that "there are not one but many Souths," and in particular three, each of which he reconstructs from the ground up. "As a result of mountains, climate, and race," he argues, "there are three societies"—the Tidewater South, Piedmont South, and Deep South—each possessing a "geographical distinctiveness" evident "in the works of fiction shaped by the various subregions."[44] In various iterations of what I call the "of course it's a construction, but . . ." argument, a self-evident, different, and autochthonous South is found, after all, to exist prior to anyone noticing and calling it that.

I argue that the notional South—the summary construct, the high-level abstraction, the common conception—doesn't come from the ground up. Rather, I claim that the that the relationship between the South in your brain and the Southeast is tenuous (and always has been), and, further, that it's deeply dependent on the intuition, as Louis Rubin puts it in *The History of Southern Literature*, that "Southern identity is important because it is." Rubin's appeal to zero-degree southernness—the group qua group—responds to a question he poses as to why, in the 1980s, American literature continues to "preserv[e] the sectional allegiances of the mid-nineteenth century." But Rubin moves in a positivist direction in a way that I won't, gesturing to an "entity within American society known as the South" important to those "who are or have been part of it."[45] That it's important, I suggest, does not require it to be an entity, at least in Rubin's sense. What Rubin does here is exactly what Barbara Garnet does: he identifies an affective attachment and assumes that it's attached to some*thing*. My approach, conversely, avoids leaping to the entity by first pausing at the meme.

The memes of Dixie, I argue, enable the circuitry of zero-degree southernness by rendering it both nontautological (by persuading us that the South *isn't just* the Southeast, that it's something *more* than an address) and inevitable (by persuading us that the South *is* the Southeast, that it emerges organically from it). In *A Turn in the South*, a Charlestonian named Marion Sass explains to V. S. Naipaul, using language that echoes Rubin's, that "Southern identity is important because it is Southern. We are Southern. That's enough." But it's not enough: he's already claimed that "Southern culture is *not simply* a matter of the agrarian culture versus the industrial, or the ideals of honor against the crass values of commerce."[46] This is a South made of memes. Having mutated and survived for nearly two centuries, southern "honor" and "agrarianism" make it possible for Sass, in the words of Bruno Latour, to render the "group definition a finite and sure thing, so finite and sure that, in the end, it looks like the object of unproblematic definition." But as Latour observes, there are endless ways to do this: "You may appeal to tradition or to law. You may invent strange hybrids like 'strategic essentialism' or entrench the boundary in 'nature.' You may even turn it into a 'genetic makeup,' associate it with 'blood and soil,' make it a 'folk tradition,' sink it into customs or habits."

As Latour suggests, group formation is a noisy, clattering enterprise. For Sass, "the agrarian culture" and the "ideals of honor" don't go without saying, which is why he says them out loud, and why, because they are useful to Naipaul's project of mapping a coherent South, they are replicated on the pages of his book. Memes *never* go without saying; reproduction and citation are essential to their function. They rarely emerge from the kind of "ensemble" that "simply lies there," having become "so unquestionable that it will be taken for granted and thus will no longer produce any trace, spark, or information," or from what Pierre Bourdieu calls a habitus, a tacit realm of reproducible practices and dispositions.[47] Rather, their reproduction produces an impression of those things. A good test of a meme, then, is a thing that ostensibly "goes without saying" but is said a lot.

The question of the relationship between what goes without saying and what's said compulsively is a vexed one, rendered even more so when "culture" is used to label different conceptions of what culture is. Culture might refer to the "complex whole" identified by Edward Burnett Tylor in 1874, "which includes knowledge, belief, art, morals, law, custom, and any other capabilities and habits acquired by man as a member of society," or to the subset of that whole constituting, as T. S. Eliot puts it, "the *whole way of life* of a people" including "all the characteristic interests and activities of a people" (but not the part of the whole shared with other peoples), or to the subset of Eliot's "way of life," which Arjun Appadurai reminds us constitutes a "virtually open-ended archive of differences," used to articulate the group's "boundary of difference," or to that subset of Appadurai's "diacritics of difference" individuals variously deploy, as Stuart Hall says, to "stabilize, fix or guarantee an unchanging 'oneness' or cultural belongingness underlying all other superficial differences."[48] (Here, a southerner might be guaranteed belongingness through her consumption of ham biscuits, even if she disliked sweet tea or preferred Korean to southern barbeque, if there is such a thing.) Is culture, then, (1) the complex whole (*all* of it, including what goes without saying), (2) the part of that whole distinctive to the group, (3) the identitarian subset of that part (the *heritage* culled from the *history*, for example), or (4) or the individually claimed part of that part?

These various definitions of culture, of course, rest on the idea that the boundaries between the society, people, or group are already self-evident, such that it is obvious where the "complex whole" ends or the "way of life" begins. Of course it isn't; hence the appeal to the Mason-Dixon line to delineate the boundary of difference as somehow geographical, despite (1) endless disputation about where the South is, exactly, (2) assurances that north Florida is southern and south Florida is northern, (3) debate over whether Appalachia is in the South or a place of its own, (4) identification of core and peripheral Souths, which assumes a default set of "southern traits" (but not always the same ones!) more prevalent in some parts of the South than in others, and (5) I could go on. In none of these is the location of the historical Mason-Dixon line in any way relevant. But then, how can we know what the group is, and thus what differences exist, until the boundary is drawn?

Rather than assume boundaries that preexist our attempts to define "culture" and "society," I accept Latour's suggestion that these terms "always have a very vague definition because it is only *when* there is a dispute, *as long as it lasts*, and *depending* on the strength exerted by dissenters that such words may receive a precise meaning. In other words, no one lives in a 'culture,' shares a 'paradigm,' or belongs to a 'society' *before* he or she clashes with others."[49] Memes are effective in such clashes because they activate what Janet Halley calls "coherentist" assumptions: "assumptions that identity inheres in group members; that group membership brings with it a uniformly shared range (or even a core) of authentic experience and attitude; and that group members are thus able to draw on their own experiences to discern those interests and establish the authority they need to speak for the group."[50] To revise Simms's claim that "to write from a people is to write a people," I proceed on the less elevated premise that to write a group is to write *as if* you're writing from a group. On this view, the South isn't just a construction; it's *under* construction (and always has been).

Representing the South as a construction doesn't really undermine the idea of "the South," as you can live in a construction—for example, any house. Conversely, we don't normally think of houses as being in arguments, but that's where the South is often located. Fredric Jameson's observation that a culture is nothing more than "the ensemble of stigmata that one group bears in the eyes of the other" is relevant to Dixie memes as they emerge amid clash and disputation, often in response to countermemes originating from "the North."[51] Less theoretically, memes can be imagined as captions in the Smudge the Cat meme, wherein the smug feline in the right-hand panel responds coolly to the overwrought woman in the left. If the Yankee woman is screaming "lazy and indolent!," the southern cat might reply that it appreciates "leisure" and a "slower pace of life." Or roles might be reversed; in proclaiming the South to be lazy, the Yankee cat may have the last word.

This claim is far from original. Nearly two decades ago, James Cobb reported that after the better part of a decade researching southern identity, "it finally dawned" on him that "historians and other observers typically defined southern peculiarities solely in relation to 'the North.'"[52] Two decades before that, Waldo W. Braden suggested that "a whole indigenous clan of images" (including the "southern way of life, southern hospitality, [and] southern womanhood") "probably won status when the natives wanted to assert their superiority over the Yankees."[53] Two decades before that, Robert Penn Warren explained how southern stigmata are "converted into badges of distinction" to be wielded against the North's "Treasury of Virtue." In this way, "laziness becomes an aesthetic sense," while "blood-lust rising from a matrix of boredom and resentful misery becomes a high sense of honor."[54] And two decades before that, W. J. Cash noted that "it was the conflict with the Yankee which really created the concept of the South as something more than a matter of geography, as an object of patriotism, in the minds of the Southerners."[55] The crucial point is that the argument (that memes are in an argument) is necessary, since southern hospitality and a slower pace of life are likely to appear as self-evident components of southern common sense.

Another problem with thinking about the South as a construction is that constructions (like houses) can seem weighty.

Cash begins with the mind of the South but also with an idea of the South as a tree with "limbs and trunk bent and twisted by the all the winds of the years, but with its tap root in the Old South." "Or better still," he continues, "it is like one of those churches one sees in England" with successive layers of architectural overlay: Roman brick, Saxon stonework, Norman arches, and Gothic superstructure.[56] The church is, in fact, a better analogy because a church isn't organic; unlike a tree, it doesn't come from the ground up. But as a *place* of worship, you can go there and kick the stone, perhaps as Dr. Johnson did to refute Bishop Berkeley. But an even better analogy, I suggest, is found in the football forever unavailable to Charlie Brown's foot. Everyone knows about the slower pace of life down south, but when you try to time it, the watch may disagree. If you try to kick a "southern sense of place," your foot will go whistling through the air. What's important here isn't whether the memes are true but that they compel belief and thereby form or maintain a body of believers.

For Cash, conversely, the mind of the South produced an actual church. Having avoided grounding his South in blood and soil, he concludes, as Michael O'Brien argues, that "the image of the planter 'actually came to be' the planter," the Word, as it were, becoming flesh and dwelling among us.[57] Cash's idealism, then, leaves the South no less solid, an outcome that in a way makes sense. Like ideas, memes have consequences; they leave their mark. Still, I'm less interested in the South as a place of worship than as an object of worship, an idea invoked by the sacred language in constructions of, say, a "certain ungeographical South-within-the-South—as portable and intangible as—as—the souls in our bodies." Imagine the communion wafer as meme. I'm less interested in what it *is*—the body of Christ? a symbol of it?—than what it *does*: consolidating a body of believers or, alternatively, dividing them into Catholics and Protestants. The church, in this view, isn't the building, but the congregation. My approach, then, is to detach memes from what they persuade us they're about (the South) and attach them to a group (some group) assembling (in some way) as southerners.

A South made of memes has a weightless feel to it, as does the idea of a South under construction. But the analogies better capture, I think, the way the South has actually operated in history: as a blueprint, as instructions for assembling a group not yet assembled or not yet fully assembled, a group in danger of dissolution or in need of repair. In simplest terms, I argue that South is, and has always been, less a matter of *where* than a matter of *who*, a group (some group) of people calling themselves southerners who, more often than not, wish to imagine themselves as emerging organically and inevitably from an unconstructed or unreconstructed where. Approaching the South in this way means listening carefully to what southerners say that the South is and, what's more, believing them (since who would know better?), but without ever believing that what they say is also true of the Southeast or that it applies to, or is intended to apply to, all persons who live there. My goal, then, is not so much to carry out a postmodernist bulldozing of the "everything is a text" variety but to show how the South has been used to assemble the group it names. I approach the South, then, as a relative term, planting myself on what Latour calls relativism's "firm ground" and insisting that the South is not a matter of fact, but of belief.[58]

A word about "Dixie." I have chosen the term purposefully and for two reasons. The first is that Dixie explicitly fantastical. It's an object of longing—a place, as I've noted elsewhere, where a certain kind of "we" wishes to "take our stand." Historically, the South didn't really start being called Dixie until it had stopped being Dixie, at which point the recollection and reproduction of Dixie proceeded apace. This unsettled relation to "the region itself" helps to keep the South in the mind and *off the ground*, helps to dis-place and dis-integrate it, which in turn allows us to better understand projects that aim to place and integrate it. The second reason is that relatively few southerners today identify with Dixie, which is increasingly associated with the bad kind of southerner who brings disrepute on the good kind of southerner. Even outside the Southeast, the stigmata are instantly legible. Dixie State University is now Utah Tech, although not without protest from the kind of people you'd suspect. And when *Vice* asks, "Why are dumb Canadians waving the Confederate flag?," we're unsurprised to find the answer is "rural weirdos."[59]

On the one hand, then, a *longing* for Dixie, an imagined land of cotton and unforgotten old times; on the other, a *disavowal* of Dixie, an imagined land of Confederate flag wavers—in neither instance signifying a place merely to be inhabited. I conclude by suggesting that the South is a bad idea, an idea we should think about *less*, and so I should like to stress early on that there is no South that is not an evolved version of Dixie, or what evolved into Dixie in the decades leading up to the Civil War. This doesn't mean that progressive southerners today are actually crypto-Confederates, although the true neo-Confederate, in fact, more reliably replicates the ideas that assembled Dixie. But it does mean that they're constructing the South out of many of the same memes. Against the notion of a fluid and dis-integrated South, then, we shall have to account for the hardy persistence of Dixie's tap root memes.

CHAPTER 1

The South under Construction

Memes of a Slaveholding People

In response to abolitionist petitions presented to Congress in January 1837, John C. Calhoun took to the Senate floor to defend the peculiar institution of the southern states. What he said of slavery—that it secured a traditional social order against radical disruption; that it could not be "subverted" without "drenching the country in blood, and extirpating one or the other of the races"; that it was the most benign form of the inevitable "conflict between labor and capital" (witness the poor houses of Europe!); that it uplifted "the black race of Central Africa"; that it was, indeed, a "positive good"— was mostly unoriginal.[1] Although Calhoun is often credited with coining the phrase, slavery, as Larry E. Tise has shown, had been described as positive good since the late eighteenth century.[2] Two things, however, had changed in the interim. First, the existence of slavery in the U.S. had evolved from a settled Constitutional question to a matter debated in the Senate. Second, Calhoun spoke not merely in defense of an institution, but on behalf of a people, a South equal to the North "in virtue, intelligence, patriotism, courage, disinterestedness, and all the high qualities which adorn our nature." Here, Calhoun was responding not just to abolitionist petitions but to his fellow senator, William Cabell Rives of Virginia, who had defended slavery on constitutional grounds but nevertheless maintained that the institution was "an evil, moral, social, and political."[3] For Calhoun, conversely, "meeting the enemy on the frontier, with a fixed determination of maintaining our position at every hazard," meant defending not just what southerners did (practice slavery, some of them), but what they were (a slaveholding people, all of them).[4]

With respect to the Old South, Allen Tate offers the sharp and brutal insight that "when one is under attack, it is inevitable that one should put not only one's best foot forward but both feet, even if one of them rests on the neck of a Negro slave."[5] In a few words, this captures the essential properties of Dixie memes during the South's initial phase of construction: they emerge within arguments and on the back foot; they are saturated with affect; they strive to return to the ground—to appear to emerge organically from an existing and inevitable state of affairs. Most crucially, they establish what Walter Benn Michaels calls the "disarticulation of difference from disagreement."[6] For Rives, defending "the constitutional rights and vital interests of the South at every hazard" didn't mean speaking on behalf of a people made different by slavery.[7] Calhoun, by contrast, ticks off the proslavery talking points but more importantly expresses "our position," insisting (before insisting that slavery is a positive good) that "*be it good or bad*, [slavery] has grown up with our society and institutions, and is so interwoven with them that to destroy it would be to destroy us as a people."[8]

After one has put both feet forward, Tate observes, "one then attributes to 'those people over there' . . . all the evil of his own world. The defensive Southerner said that *if only* 'those people over there' would let us alone, the vast Sabine Farm of the South (where men read Horace but did not think it necessary to be Horace) would perpetuate itself forever."[9] Here, Tate seems to decode the southern Sabine Farm as a retort made to "those people over there," not as a pastoral enclave free of political contention. But Tate was himself a defensive southerner and a poet as well, comfortable in the latter capacity with what he calls "the fundamental conflicts that cannot be logically resolved."[10] Of the plantation myth, he insists that he uses "the word myth not to indicate a fantasy, but a reality." "The South," he notes, "was an aggregate of farms and plantations, presided over by our composite Agrarian hero, Cicero Cincinnatus. I can think of no better image for what the South was before 1860, and for what it largely still was until about 1914, than that of the old gentleman in Kentucky who sat every afternoon in his front yard under an old sugar tree, reading Cicero's Letters to Atticus."[11] Even as composite, the image of the agrarian hero is preposterously specific but yet familiar enough to represent, for Tate and possibly for us, an idea of "what the South was" that has perpetuated itself for nearly two centuries. Missing from the image is the foot resting "on the neck of the Negro slave."

Like many Dixie memes, Cicero Cincinnatus is a mutation of slavery as a positive good. The plantation over which he presides, aggregated into "the South" *through the image*, is a familiar one, replicated millions of times and long outlasting the arguments from which it emerged. No one in 1914, Tate's expiration date for "what the South was," was arguing that slavery was a positive good, although the image of the plantation continued—and continues today—to tell us something significant about the South. I've argued that segregating the South from the Southeast allows us to isolate the former in its strict capacity as the basis of group formation. Memes act as the flag around which the group is enjoined to rally. But to complicate the analogy, if memes act as flags, they often seem like photographs, while, in turn, photographs can serve as flags. In 1859, it would have been theoretically possible to photograph a plantation owner reading Cicero under an old sugar tree. A nontrivial number of such persons no doubt existed. The fecundity of the meme, however, has little to do with how accurately it represents the region and much to do with its power to aggregate southerners.

The word "myth" lures us in the direction of representation in way that I want to avoid. A myth might misrepresent reality ("that's just a myth"), or it might represent a different order of reality. In his classic analysis of myth, Roland Barthes identifies a two-layer semiological system wherein a photograph of "a young Negro in a French uniform . . . saluting, with his eyes uplifted, probably fixed on a fold of the tricolor" signifies both a meaning ("a Negro is giving a French salute") and, "on the plane of myth," a "*form*" (or concept), namely, that "France is a great Empire, that all her sons, without any color discrimination, faithfully serve under her flag, and that there is no better answer to the detractors of an alleged colonialism than the zeal shown by this Negro in serving his so-called oppressors." The photograph acts, then, as a flag, and in two specific ways relevant to my analysis. First, it terminates in what Barthes calls a "formless, unstable, nebulous condensation"; the "knowledge contained in a mythical concept," he insists, "is confused, made of yielding, shapeless associations." Second, such "unity and coherence" as it does possess are "above all due to its function." For Barthes, the "fundamental character of the mythical concept is to be *appropriated*"—in this instance to "appeal to such and such a group of readers and not another" and, more specifically, to the readers of *Paris Match*, a right-wing magazine supporting French imperialism as a positive good.[12] The contingent and dialogic nature of memes also contributes to the photograph's ability to serve as a flag. The image of Barthes's soldier assembles a particular group of Frenchmen with around a contested (if formless) idea of France, and it does so in competition with other groups holding different ideas. The meme, in other words, *depends* on other words—in this instance, allegations of colonialism and "so-called" oppression. (The invocation of "so called" tells us that a meme is in the vicinity: it's called that by *them*, but *we* call it this. Scare quotes and italics often do similar work.)

But just as this vague and formless idea of France has little to do with the political rivalries of Provence, the novels of Victor Hugo, or the customs and habits of Parisian diners, so, I suggest, the original memes of Dixie bear a tenuous relation to the region they purport to represent. Indeed, the passage of time renders the observation supererogatory. Few would argue today that Cicero Cincinnatus, a figure vaguely associated with heat, a classical tradition, leisure, and benevolent paternalism (since he interrupts his reading only when the "hands . . . in the adjoining field needed orders") tells us much about the slave labor camp over which he presided.[13] The same is true of his adjuncts within the plantation memeplex, both those included among the southern people (the belle, the lady) and those who, like Barthes's soldier, were made to salute their "so-called oppressors" (the mammy, the uncle). Fewer still would deny that Dixie memes emerged within a heated debate, usually with an imagined interlocutor called "the North." But to the extent that memes persuade us that they are representations (even misrepresentations) of the South or defenses of the South, they persuade us that there is a South being represented or defended. As John Shelton Reed argues the point in *One South*, to concede that the South is various, contradictory, and hard to explain is "not to deny that it exists, but rather presupposes that there is something there to talk about."[14]

That is precisely the presupposition that I wish to avoid, at least insofar as a *there* (rather than a *who*) is concerned. After all, there is also plenty of talk about alien invaders and Pizzagate, both of which illustrate important properties of memes: (1) they replicate not because they correspond to reality but because they pay a psychological wage high enough to persuade your brain to host them, and (2) they are good at assembling groups, especially groups under threat, that will, in turn, replicate the meme.[15] To view memes simply as a way insiders or outsiders represent or "argue" a prior social reality—an already assembled state of affairs, be it a "way of life," a civilization, a race, a culture, or a people—is to presume the group so constituted and thus to render it a foregone conclusion. And yet prior to the act of what Tate describes as putting the best southern foot forward, there's no southern foot to speak of, no line separating the southern group from "those people over there." There's also no possibility of keeping others *in line* by citing coherentist principles that authorize the individual to speak for the group.

In the decades leading up to the Civil War, descriptive statements about the South increasingly embedded the sentiments and obligations binding all true southerners. Describing what the South *was* shaded imperceptibly into accounts of what the South *ought* to be. In 1862, William Gladstone observed from Britain that "there is no doubt that Jefferson Davis and other leaders of the South have made an army; they are making, it appears, a navy; and they have made what is more than either, they have made a nation."[16] But what was the nation made of? Lacking a literature (as everyone conceded), what formed the imagined community for which hundreds of thousands of southerners were willing to fight and die? A partial and indirect answer can be found in Walter Hines Page's novel *The Southerner* (1909), whose protagonist claims that in North Carolina,

> traditions had long been accepted as facts. Society "before the war" was thought, even by men whose lives ran back into that period, to be very different from what it really was. A few phrases about "cavaliers" and "great planters" had made a picture in the public mind that, so far as our State was concerned, was wholly untrue. The prevalent notion of the Civil War, fostered by the Veterans and the Daughters, was erroneous. The real character of General Lee was misunderstood. His name was worshipped, but his real opinions were unknown and had been curiously distorted. . . . The people did not know their own story.

If you're following my argument, those "few phrases" and the sacred name of General Lee *constitute* the people's story, circa 1909, by causing them to think of themselves as a people. In trying to eliminate that story with facts (the least effective way), Page is simply trying to assemble a different group, which he attempts, in part, by identifying Confederate veterans as apparitions. "They were dead men," the protagonist asserts, "most of them, moving around the living as ghosts; and yet, as ghosts in a play, they held the stage."[17] But Page's hope of killing off the Confederate undead neglects the fecundity of the "few phrases about 'cavaliers' and 'great planters'" that not only survived to his own day but had helped to assemble the Army of Northern Virginia.

"Cavalier" was one way of making a "picture in the public mind" that installed the great planter as the representative of a slaveholding people. Invariably, it stood opposite "Yankee," "Puritan," or "Roundhead," the favored memes designating "those people over there." (As a general rule, Puritans, who were fanatical, were worse than Yankees, who, at their best, were merely moneygrubbing and common. Roundheads were worst of all.) Upon the outbreak of the war, the British observer Samuel Phillips Day reports that "the prevailing idea throughout the Confederate States was to 'whip the Yankees.'" In an effort to align his British audience with the southern cause, Day draws heavily on the Cavalier legend, finding abundant evidence that "the Cavalier of the South" had transplanted British civilization to the New World and in so doing provided "an agreeable contrast" to the "New England Puritan." Had a writer recently claimed that Virginia was settled "by the great Anglo-Saxon family, whose swords were never drawn in vain, and before whom the hosts of the Cavaliers in the Old World were driven off as chaff before the wind?" Then that writer had clearly "fallen into an error."[18]

Day might have had in mind someone like Hugh Blair Grigsby, a wealthy Tidewater planter descended from the First Families of Virginia, as representative of a present-day Cavalier. But Grigsby was, in fact, the writer in error. In an 1855 speech on the Virginia Convention of 1776, Grigsby looked "with contempt on that miserable figment, which has so long held a place in our histories, which seeks to trace the distinguishing and salient points of the Virginia character to the influence of those butterflies of the British aristocracy." For Grigsby, this association would compromise the particular glory of Revolutionary Virginia: that, out of sheer principle, it had "led the van in sustaining the common rights of the colonies," even though it was "attached to the parent country" and possessed a "genial soil." By contrast, the northern colonies, "occupying a sterile soil, were compelled, in self-defense, to engage in commerce and manufactures." "Self-defense" tells us that northern manufacturing was inferior to Virginia agrarianism, but Grigsby required no Cavalier to buttress the glory of what was, in fact, "a great Anglo-Saxon people placed in a position of all others best adapted to the full and generous development of their particular virtues." The Cavalier was simply unfit to take advantage: "A home in the wilderness, to be cleared by his own axe, and guarded by his own musket against a wily foe, was no place for the voluptuary and the idler."[19] Nearly a century later, W. J. Cash argues in terms precisely echoing Grigsby's that wresting land "from the forest and the intractable red man" was a "harsh and bloody task, wholly unsuited to the talents" of the gentleman. For Cash, this disproved the "Cavalier thesis," which he claims "nobody any longer holds . . . in its overt form," although he goes on to complain that the "popular mind still clings to it in its essence."[20] According to Daniel Singal in 1982, twentieth-century southern intellectuals, including himself, had little choice but to confront the myth, so fully had the Cavalier "become the very symbol of the South, intimately bound up with the region's sense of identity, providing southerners with their predominant source of common pride in the perpetual struggle with Yankeedom."[21]

Against such efforts to exterminate it, the persistence of the Cavalier meme in the "popular mind" suggests that it is good at assembling groups, including a Confederate army eager to "whip the Yankees" and, in time, a southern people who had received the whipping. This defeat is mournfully evoked in a song performed by a character in Charles Wells Russell's 1866 novel *Roebuck*:

> The lance of chivalry is broke, its iron mail is rust,
> But knightly truth and courage live when knights have turned
>   to dust:
> There never rode a truer knight in battle or career
> Than this grey-coated gentleman, the Southern Cavalier.[22]

The lyric imagines Confederate soldiers as knightly Cavaliers, but did they imagine themselves that way? Few had descended from the English aristocracy; all lacked lances; many did not own a horse.

Before considering how Cavalier and Yankee evolved to define and maintain a group boundary, I want to briefly turn to two ways of thinking about the Cavalier that places him on the ground rather than where I suggest he belongs (in an argument between groups). The first (positivist) view maintains that a quantum of Cavalierness was already present in the habitus and therefore that marking the group merely required simple observation. As advanced by David Hackett Fischer in *Albion's Seed*, this argument—basically, that the Cavalier was photograph, not flag—is largely unconvincing. Even if different British "folkways" were, as Fischer argues, imported into the colonies by different population groups— East Anglian Puritans settling in Massachusetts, royalists settling in Virginia, and so forth—it does not follow that a difference in habitus was a significant factor in group formation in the decades leading up to war. Fischer, for example, argues that the gentlemen of royalist Virginia "were encouraged by the customs of the country to maintain a predatory attitude toward women" and thus that the abolitionist "indictment of slavery for its association with predatory sex"—over a century later—"had a solid foundation in historical fact."[23] The historical fact of sexual predation was solid, its Cavalier origin less so, since planters of Scots-Irish (and even Yankee) stock were no less prone to sexual predation. But what offended abolitionists was the fact of sexual predation, not its Cavalier origin. Nor did they object to the purported Cavalier origins of a slaveholding people but rather to the fact that they practiced slavery. For their part, no apologist for slavery defended sexual predation as an aristocratic prerogative. In short, the Cavalier was not causally implicated in the argument over slavery; rather, the figure evolved to mark a difference between the groups engaged in that argument. For Virginians, and eventually for southerners, the Cavalier was simply a way of putting a best foot forward, of rendering inevitable, because it was genealogical, the character of a slave-holding people.

On the idealist view, by contrast, the Cavalier does not emerge organically from an unmarked culture; instead, as Cash maintains, the image of the planter *becomes* the planter. Since the Cavalier per se was difficult to render in the flesh, we are forced to turn to adjacent memes to consider how the image of the Cavalier came to define southerners. The Cavalier was a chevalier, which was associated with chivalry, knighthood, and a medieval world feudal in character. An early version of the idealist argument appears in Mark Twain's *Life on the Mississippi*, which attributes the South's "sham chivalries" to the viral "enchantments" of Sir Walter Scott. In his diagnosis of the "Sir Walter Disease," Twain argues that the infectious nature of Scott's ideas altered "the character of the Southerner, or Southron, according to Sir Walter's starchier way of phrasing it." He notes that while both the southerner of the American Revolution and the southerner of the Civil War owned slaves "the former resembles the latter as an Englishman resembles a Frenchman."[24] Eugene Genovese and Elizabeth Fox-Genovese observe that the constellated chivalry/knight/feudalism idea produced, from the 1840s forward, hundreds of jousting contests throughout the region.[25] Was this not, then, part of the world, the actual world, that the slaveholders made? I am partially sympathetic to the argument, since in replicating memes leave their mark. Just as thousand copies of a print stereotype might coalesce into a notional stereotype, so replicating an event borrowed from Scott's novels might create the impression of a chivalric people. To be enjoined, as were the "Sir Knights" at an 1854 ring tournament in Hugenot Springs, Virginia, to "repel the sanguinary chivalry of Gothic barbarism" and the "ludicrous chivalry of Quixotic caprice" but to "vindicate the true chivalry of the age in which you live" was to be asked to import an ideal into the quotidian world of the nineteenth century.[26] A thousand readings of Scott's novels might produce three plantations with names borrowed from them and a further hundred print impressions of the word "southron," a term that competed with "southerner" from the 1840s through the 1860s.

But just as southerners didn't joust because they had always done so, neither, I suggest, did they joust because at some point jousting had become an organic custom—a thing that went without saying. Indeed, the spectacle of the joust appeared to Daniel R. Hundley of Alabama to be not a folkway but a joke. Writing a year before he joined the Confederate Army, Hundley mockingly asks his reader to "note well with what a cavalier-like grace" the "modern Cotton Knight . . . ambles daintily forward on the back of a docile gelding, holding a sharpened stick under his arm, and gallantly and gloriously endeavoring to thrust the same through an iron ring!"[27] Kwame Anthony Appiah argues that the lies that bind find their way into the habitus by entraining norms associated with identities, but surely "vindicating the true chivalry" had less to do with unconscious habits and dispositions than with delineating a group boundary.[28] In any event, it is *only* in disputation that such notions acquired their group-forming character—only, that is, when the Cavalier was arrayed opposite the Yankee, Puritan, or Roundhead or when it was made known that chivalry was unknown in the North.

In fact, the Cavalier meme appears, as with ring tournaments themselves, only in the few decades leading up to the Civil War, closely paralleling the intensification of the slavery controversy. The idea was of no use to Revolutionary Virginia, and it was altogether unknown to the colonial period preceding it. Michael O'Brien finds the rudiments of the Cavalier myth to take shape in John Pendleton Kennedy's *Swallow Barn* (1832), which includes a satirical chapter titled "Traces of the Feudal System" in the Old Dominion and smiles outright at the character of Ned Hazard, who returns from an escapade "as knight errant" in the quarrels of South America as "the most disquixotted cavalier that ever hung up his shield of a scurvy crusade."[29] But a developed Cavalier myth, he argues, appears only in William Alexander Caruthers's *The Cavaliers of Virginia* (1834), which identifies the group as "the first founders of the aristocracy which prevails in Virginia to this day" and "the immediate ancestors of that generous fox-hunting, wine-drinking, duelling and reckless race of men, which gives so distinct a character to Virginians wherever they may be found."[30]

Given the Cavalier's relatively late appearance in a just a handful of novels, it is likely that only a very few southerners could, in 1840, provide even the "few phrases" Page associates with the meme. True, in 1839, Congressman Henry A. Wise of Virginia defended his participation in a duel by proclaiming, "I belong to the class of the Cavaliers, not to the Roundheads!"[31] And two years earlier fellow Virginian Abel Upshur had denounced the political machinations of northern "fanatics," denying any "true affinity between the Roundhead and the Cavalier."[32] But for Grigsby, who knew Virginia history better than either of them, the Cavalier myth was mere mythology. Nor was it clear that the figure resonated beyond the state line. Calvin H. Wiley of North Carolina doubted that the Cavalier, or even the South, was relevant to his state. In his 1851 *North Carolina Reader*, he attempts what Page's fictional protagonist would attempt two generations hence: to tell the story of a people free of Cavaliers. "New England gathered to herself the Puritans," Wiley claims, while "the emigrant courtiers and cavaliers steered for Virginia and South-Carolina." Given its "robust modesty, its capacity for equality," North Carolina required a wholly different effort to "fix on common objects the affections of the public." Indeed, Wiley declares North Carolina a "land between extremes," exempt from not only from the "gloomy fanaticism and chilling selfishness of the north" but also "the bloody scenes and blazing passions of the South."[33] Of South Carolina's Cavalier roots, William Henry Trescot was similarly skeptical. "There was very little of the Cavalier element in the settlement of this State," he claims, and "the spirit of chivalry . . . infused no romance in our settlement."[34]

The Cavalier, then, consolidated an idea of the South only in fits and starts, even as it increasingly persuaded Americans, as William Taylor argues in *Cavalier and Yankee*, to "look upon their society and culture as divided between a North and a South, a democratic, commercial civilization and an aristocratic, agrarian one."[35] But there was much commercialism and democracy in the Southeast and many farms in the North.[36] As Taylor shows, the Cavalier proved attractive to northern elites fearful of populist movements and dependent on southern trade.[37] Other factors impeded the integration of a single, notional South. For Trescot, as for many, any American's "home instincts and affections" were "bounded by State lines," and the states did not always get along.[38] The Virginian, according to Joseph Glover Baldwin, did not reproach "the poor Carolinian and Tennesseeian . . . with his misfortune of birthplace," thinking "the affliction . . . enough without the triumph."[39] For Carolinians like Wiley, the feeling was mutual. "The South," in its hypostatized and agential form, competed unevenly with a South that was merely geographical, a region often rendered as "the southern states" or, as *De Bow's* has it, the "southern and western" states.[40] It was not always clear that the people of the Southeast were a single people, nor that a person living there was either a southerner or a southron—that is, a kind of person.

Such clarity—or misprision—would increase as the slavery controversy intensified, and the Cavalier would appear more frequently to mark the difference between the North and the South.[41] By the second year of the war, it was evident to the *Richmond Whig* and its readership that "war for Southern independence" was a "war of races" between the Puritan, the "ultra liberty man of the world" given to anarchy and misrule, and the "Cavalier, or higher Norman type," destined "to be the ruling power in any country." The history of the United States had shown this to be so. The Cavalier had dominated the presidency; prior to Lincoln, the few "Puritan presidents had been under the control of the Southern mind throughout their administrations," and, "of course, all of the [United States'] advancement and glory has been from the Southern mind."[42] The "antithesis between the Puritan and the Cavalier," had come, as Trescot observes, to be a thing "we hear constantly," whatever its basis in history or relevance to the state of South Carolina.[43] Through such iteration, the Cavalier had, within the space of a few decades, evolved into a thing many southerners knew because they knew it, thus marking an absolute and familiar difference between South and North. A notion of Cavalierness may have trickled down, influencing the way a Confederate soldier stood astride his horse, grounding his belief that he could whip seven, ten, or twenty Yankees (according to, respectively, an 1864 arithmetic primer from North Carolina, General John B. Hood, and one of the Tarleton brothers in the film version of *Gone with the Wind*), or even shaping the way he imagined his ancestors.[44] But it definitely told him that he belonged to a group to which the Cavalier was significant in a vague way. And if this amounted to little more than Page's few phrases, the Cavalier told him not just what team he was on (as it does for a guard on the University of Virginia basketball team) but that his team was different from the enemy team and superior to it.

The Nature of a Slaveholding People

The Cavalier was but one way in which the South came to seem both self-evident and inevitable. Blood, soil, and climate were also said to have produced a distinctive way of life characterized by leisure, hospitality, and fine manners, "cultural traits" (as we now call them) most conspicuously on display on the plantation, which evolved into what Edgar Thompson calls "the molecular unit, the very quintessence, of the South and of southernism" and was where the South appeared most often.[45] The dividing line between peoples, as John Calhoun had foreseen in 1837, was drawn by the peculiar institution— peculiar not because it was strange but because it was distinctive to the southern states. Including "under the Southern all the slaveholding States," Calhoun identifies the difference underlying all other differences between North and South.[46] As Thomas Jefferson foresaw in 1820, the "geographical line" marked by slavery, "once conceived and held up to the angry passions of men, will never be obliterated; and every new irritation will mark it deeper and deeper."[47] Calhoun echoes the point, although the angry passions, in his view, existed only on the other side. Although it had "infected" neither the Senate nor "the great mass of the intelligent and business portion of the North," an "incendiary spirit" had spread, and would continue to do so—through the pulpit, schools, and press, "those great instruments by which the mind of the rising generation will be formed."[48]

A different, but equally incendiary, spirit emerged in the mind of the South, eventuating, briefly, in a nation-state explicitly founded in the institution. The Confederacy's Constitution, Alexander Stephens proclaims in his 1862 "Corner-Stone Speech," had settled "*forever*, all the agitating questions relating to our peculiar institution—African slavery as it exists amongst us." "Our new [Confederate] government," he claims, "rests upon the great truth that the negro is not equal to the white man; that slavery—subordination to the superior race—is his natural and normal condition."[49] But for all the emphasis on the centrality of the institution, a slaveholding people did not consist merely of persons who had chosen or were entitled to hold slaves. For every explicit articulation of slavery as a foundational and positive good, for every insistence that it was an *institution* and not an *interest* (which was what the Yankees had), there was another that built the inevitability of the group around softer, adjacent memes, assigning group difference to matters beyond mere politics. These memes allowed the South to survive the destruction of its foundation, but in their formation, the dispute over slavery always lingered on the horizon.

There were many ways of locating group difference in nature. Jefferson's "geographical line" was marked with the passions of men, but it could also be found on a map. In 1850,

Trescot disavows any need for a "vindication of slavery" by declaring the institution beyond argument:

> We know that Providence has placed us in the midst of an institution which we cannot, as we value national existence, destroy. . . . [Slavery] informs all our habits of thought, lies at the basis of our political faith and of our social existence. In a word, for all that we are, we believe ourselves, under God, indebted to the institution of slavery—for a national existence, a well ordered liberty, a prosperous agriculture, and exulting commerce, a free people, and a firm government. And where God has placed us, there, without argument, are we resolved to remain.

God had placed this people in the midst of an institution and nature helped, "discharg[ing] God's great commission—to divide the nations." Even "the most superficial review" of the U.S. map revealed that "nature itself has drawn deeply the sectional lines." History, he insists, had "followed their guidance" to preserve the "antithesis of Plymouth and Jamestown."[50]

Although few found Trescot's geography persuasive, climate proved more reliable in differentiating peoples. The idea that nations came from nature was a staple of romantic nationalism and by no means peculiar to the South. In his *History of English Literature*, Hippolyte Taine attributes the differences "for the most part" between the German races, on the one hand, and the Greek and Latin races, on the other, to climate. The former inhabited "cold and moist lands, deep in black marshy forests or on the shores of a wild ocean, caged in by melancholy or violent sensations." The latter, inhabiting "a lovely landscape," were "inclined from the beginning to social ways, to a settled organization of the state, to feelings and dispositions such as develop the art of oratory, the talent for enjoyment, the inventions of science, letters, arts."[51] Taine, a member of Team Greek and Latin, prefers the "lovely landscape" for reasons that southerners too preferred it. A "culture of chivalry," for example, could scarcely "propogate [*sic*] under the chilly skies" of New York, where "the good people of the Empire State ogled it, smelt it, and even kissed it, but the chivalry sickened and faded away."[52]

Unsurprisingly, writers from colder climes disputed the hierarchy. These included John George Metcalf, a physician who remarks that it is "passing strange" that the "hardy sons of New-England should exchange the bracing air of their native hills and their variegated landscape, for the pestilential breezes and pine-barrens of Carolina." "But there is magic," he continues, "in the two words, sunny South; and it is the romance of this expression which operates almost with the power of enchantment. It is this talismanic phrase which entices so many of our citizens . . . from the pure moral land of the Pilgrims, to swell the annual harvest for the garner of death in this same sunny South."[53] The epithet "sunny South," which would survive the war, marked for southerners a land and people gifted by nature. A. B. Meek's "Girl of the Sunny South," for example, is a lass "bright as thy native clime" and "cinctured by light divine," while in *The Sunny South; Or, the Southerner at Home* (1860) "a Northern governess" ostensibly documents the "romantic features of Southern rural life on the tobacco, cotton, and sugar estates: the three forms under which true Southern Life presents itself."[54] But the phrase functioned reliably as a disputed meme and could signal, as for the abolitionist poet Elizur Wright Jr., a landscape of depravity:

> Oh sunny South! how can it be,
> Thy soil, which ay with plenty waves,—
> In one year gives the fruit of three
> Should drink the tears and blood of slaves?[55]

Heat, more broadly, was associated with dissolution and violence. According to Ralph Waldo Emerson, "the highest civility has never loved the hot zones. Wherever snow falls, there is usually civil freedom. Where the banana grows, the animal system is indolent and pampered at the cost of higher qualities: the man is grasping, sensual, and cruel." Although free of bananas, the South was, in Emerson's estimation, surfeited with sensuality and cruelty, a "country . . . not civil, but barbarous" where "liberty is attacked in the primary institution of their social life."[56]

Spokesmen for the South, by contrast, saw heat as positively connected to the "primary institution." Reviewing in 1859 Charles Mackay's *Life and Liberty in America*, George Fitzhugh complains of Mackay's "prejudices against southern climates." Claiming that "cold benumbs and renders inert the mental and physical faculties," Fitzhugh explains that "heat stimulates them into action." This accounted for both the indolence of the "stupid, benumbed and torpid" peoples of northern Europe and Asia and the "industry, intelligence, and enterprise" of Athens, Persia, and Rome. "Every line of history," Fitzhugh insists, "refutes our author's doctrine that slavery and the southern climate enervates national character," since "all the great peoples of the world have not only been southerners, but slaveholders, also."[57] Thomas Jefferson also associated slavery and heat but didn't intimate it made southerners great. "In a warm climate," he explains, "no man will labour for himself who can make another labour for him," adding that a "greater degree of transpiration renders [Blacks] more tolerant of heat, and less so of cold than the whites."[58] The idea evolved to sanction the racial division of labor. Senator John Rowan of Kentucky, whose plantation would later be celebrated in "My Old Kentucky Home," asserted in 1830 that "in Southern climates, nothing is so much dreaded as exposure to the fervid rays of the sun." Echoing Jefferson, he comes to a different conclusion:

> In such a climate none will labor constantly, but those who are forced to do so. . . . The languor of the climate disqualifies them to conquer their condition, and fits them for it; and, owing to the bounty of nature, the labor of a comparatively small portion of the people will support them all. Those who do not labor, while they enjoy the refreshing influence of the shade, are left in possession of liberty, with leisure to cultivate its theory, and contemplate its charms, until they become enamoured of it.

Finding "no instance on record, of a Southern people being, and continuing to be free, who did not tolerate slavery,"

Rowan enjoins his "Northern brethren" to concede that "nature extracts from the people of the South the toleration of slavery, as the only condition upon which they can themselves be free."[59]

In a public letter to Secretary of State Daniel Webster, New Orleans physician Samuel A. Cartwright invokes science to argue that "negro slavery, from natural laws, if not interfered with, must ultimately be confined to that region of country South, where, from the heat of the climate and the nature of the cultivation, negro labor is more efficient, cheaper, and more to be relied on than white labor." Work that for whites would result in "disease and death" "proves to be only a wholesome and beneficial exercise to the negro, awakening him from his natural torpor to a new life of pleasure and activity." To prevent dissolution of the Union, why not, Cartwright asks, "give the whole subject up to the higher law of Nature to regulate?"[60] For Cartwright, nature's climate spoke with the authority of nature's God: the Bible "declares the same thing, as it gave [the negro] the significant name *Canaan* (or '*Submissive knee bender*') to express his nature, and doomed him to slavery, as a condition the most consonant to that nature."[61] For Jefferson it was different: slavery caused him to tremble when he reflected that God was just, while a warm climate encouraged the decay of morals and industry. "Of the proprietors of slaves," he complains, "a very small proportion indeed are ever seen to labour."[62]

Heat, then, was used to explain both the presence of slavery and the character of a slaveholding people. For Fitzhugh, heat made southerners the "most industrious, the most enterprising, the greatest people in the world," but the long-term trend vindicated Rowan, for whom heat made southerners languorous and leisurely. This is the South of "My Old Kentucky Home," where "the darkies are gay," of Tate's Cicero Cincinnatus reading Cicero under a sugar tree, and of U. B. Phillips's *Life and Labor in the Old South* (1929), which begins "by discussing the weather, for that has been the chief agency in making the South distinctive." "In the tedious heat,"

Phillips explains, "work is hard; indolence easy; speech is likely to be slow and somewhat slurred; manners are soft; and except when tempers are hot, the trend is toward easy-going practices even among healthy people."[63] In explaining that the character of a slaveholding people had been shaped by climate, Phillips followed numerous commentators of the nineteenth century for whom the idea of leisure and its adjacent memes (hospitality, manners, refinement) softened the hard sell of slavery as a positive good by presenting it as an organically evolved system easily accommodated within the Union.

As a separate and different world, it could be known only from the inside. Just as the "inhabitant of the interesting but unknown country of Oregon" possessed, because he had been there, authority to profess of "its soil and climate," so the southerner, Nathaniel Beverley Tucker argues, should be heard out on the matter of slavery. From within slavery's habitat, it was clear to Tucker that divine love had brought together "two races before divided by the strongest antipathies." Just as Isaiah had prophesied that "the lion shall eat straw like the ox," so had the hearts of "the lordly white lion of Caucasus" and "the patient negro ox" been "knit[ted] together in love."[64]

Hospitality was important because it eased the ingress of the stranger to this different world. Ideally, the encounter would show evidence of affection, or at least accommodation, between master and servant. Frank Meriwether, owner of the titular plantation in Kennedy's *Swallow Barn*, is particularly gratified "to pick up any genteel stranger within the purlieus of Swallow Barn, and put him to the proof of a week's hospitality, if it only be for the pleasure of exercising his rhetoric upon him." "He is a kind master," the narrator remarks, "and considerate toward his dependants, for which reason, although he owns many slaves, they hold him in profound reverence, and are very happy under dominion."[65] The suggestive connection between hospitality and paternalistic benevolence reappears in "The Night Funeral of a Slave," a piece reprinted in *De Bow's Review* in 1856. In it, a traveler "from a colder clime" visits Georgia, having, he says, "brought with me all the prejudices which so generally prevail in the free States in regard to this 'institution.'" Welcomed by a planter "in the true spirit of southern hospitality," he finds that the man is mourning the death of his "truest and most reliable friend," a "faithful servant" whose dying words had been "Master, meet me in heaven." After witnessing an unexpectedly lavish funeral, the traveler concludes that he "shall return to my Northern home, deeply impressed with the belief, that dispensing with the *name* of freedom, the negroes of the South are the happiest and most contented people on the face of the earth."[66]

As Anthony Szczesiul thoroughly demonstrates in *The Southern Hospitality Myth*, the idea of southern hospitality emerged not in a disinterested effort to distinguish South from North but within an argument over slavery. An image from the *American Anti-Slavery Almanac* for 1839, for example, depicts a lavish feast with an enslaved person appearing in the far background. Captioned "Southern Arguments to Stop the Mouths of Northern Guests," it represents southern hospitality, in Szczesiul's words, as "nothing more than performative propaganda designed to enlist northerners in the cause of slavery," a charge "made repeatedly by abolitionists from the 1830s up until the Civil War."[67] The propaganda of "The Night Funeral of a Slave," for example, is answered by *The Liberator*, which counters that the ceremony was designed to divert the attention of the enslaved away from the fact that "these funeral expenses, so *kindly given* by the master, have been earned, a thousand times over, by the unpaid labor of the deceased slave." Hiring a minister to preach that "heaven is the reward of patient, submissive, unreasoning industry" persuaded the enslaved to accept their condition, thus preventing the need for "chains and the lash."[68]

While "the lash" (a pervasive synecdoche of slavery's moral depravity) signaled the whipping post, hospitality attached itself to the column and the front porch, a space where groups made different by slavery might gather together. In 1840, the

Philadelphia Repository notes that when it came to hospitality, there was a "wonderful contrast" between the North and the South. In the North, it was a "thing unknown," while in the South, it was offered by "refined society" to the "stranger . . . wherever he goes." Dismissing the idea that the difference is merely an artifact of Puritan and Cavalier heritage, the *Repository* identifies "the influence of slavery" as "the real cause of all the difference." Surplus slave labor—"numerous servants" having "little more than half employment"—leaves the master's "time . . . almost entirely at his own disposal" and permits the ladies of the household to "devote themselves to the entertainment of their guests . . . almost without intermission."[69] Historians have questioned whether there was such a surplus of leisure as described in these accounts, and their suspicions are supported by *De Bow's*, for example, worrying in 1853 that although "hospitality is proverbial," the "untiring ambition to make money prevents much sociable intercourse."[70] But the proverb survived to mediate between South and North. In 1859, the Richmond *Daily Dispatch* hopes that the "testimony" of northerners "in regard to southern hospitality" might "add new and powerful links to our national union," adding that "the true character of a people can never be understood until they are seen at their own homes."[71] Adopting a different tactic, T. Pollock Burgwyn wrote in 1849 to the editor of the *American Farmer* inviting him to visit the "*baronial estates* on the James river—estates that many a German or Italian prince would now freely barter his principality for." There, Burgwyn promised, planters "would greet you with (I will not here use the vaunted expression we Southerners are so apt to indulge in, to wit, 'true Southern hospitality,' since I can bear evidence to having seen as much of that at the North as at the South) a Farmer's welcome, and with their accustomed hospitality."[72]

If hospitality allowed the South to put a best foot forward, there was also a defensive quality to the idea. Hospitality came with the expectation of reciprocal kindness, which, when not forthcoming, often occasioned rage. Responding to the "ti-

rade against slavery" offered by Swedish novelist Fredrika
Bremer, the *Daily Dispatch* of Richmond inveighs against the
"heinous . . . ingratitude of the creatures who bask in the sun-
shine of Southern hospitality, and repay its pleasant warmth
by the venom of the serpent."[73] In *Social Relations in Our
Southern States*, Hundley similarly denounces Frederick Law
Olmsted, whose southern travel narratives describe a region
benighted by slavery. Olmstead, Hundley remarks, was one
of a class of "lying, sneaking, cowardly knaves, foot-padding
it all through the Southern States, endeavoring by every devilish machination to kindle the fires of a servile insurrection,
and writing calumnious letters to Northern newspapers, of-
tentimes defaming the characters of the unsuspecting patrons,
at whose hospitable board their miserable carcasses are each
day filled with abundance of every species of good cheer."[74]
Fictional variants of the scenario were common. The narrator of Joseph M. Field's "A Lyncher's Own Story" (1845) offers his home to "any stranger wishing to put up" if he is "an
honest looking white man" but repays the "treachery" of a
disguised abolitionist by lynching him.[75] Similarly, the planter
of Caroline Lee Hentz's *Planter's Northern Bride* (1854) is
stung by the "ingratitude and treachery" of the "*holy* traitor" Brainard, an abolitionist minister who "had so basely
requited his hospitality and confidence" by winding "coils"
around the "necks of his deluded victims"—enslaved persons
"seduced" into aspirations of freedom.[76]

Often, hospitality responded to criticisms of southern
shabbiness and economic backwardness. These, in turn, were
often attributed to "the curse of slavery"—a ubiquitous term,
according to Virginia governor John B. Floyd, of "deep and
bitter reproach which the fanatics of the North heap upon
the South, as being disfigured with the 'blot of African bond-
age'—a land withering under the 'curse of slavery.'"[77] The
curse had both economic and moral dimensions. Emphasizing
the latter, the Reverend Horace Bushnell of Hartford, Con-
necticut, concedes that in the southern colonies, "slavery set
the masters at once on a footing of ease, gave them leisure for

elegant intercourse, for unprofessional studies, and seasoned their character thus with that kind of cultivation which distinguishes men of society." But slavery, being "a condition against nature," has therefore "the curse of nature . . . on it, and it bows to its doom, by a law as irresistible as gravity." "However highly we may estimate the humanizing power of hospitality," Bushnell concludes, "it cannot be regarded as any sufficient spring of character."[78] Of Yankees less knavish than Olmsted, Hundley observes that "accustomed from infancy to hear and read of Southern hospitality and wealth, as well as of the splendors of natural scenery in all Southern latitudes," they cannot "refrain at times from expressing their disappointment, when they come to realize the facts." Of a particular traveler, he writes, "it was still plain as a pikestaff that in his own mind he connected the vast solitude, in the awful stillness whereof he seemed to be dying, with the 'curse of slavery.'" Hundley corrects the misprision, noting that the northern traveler "passing by a princely plantation—hid from view though it be by the dense forest of the river's bank— whose proprietor could with a single year's crop buy up half-a-dozen New England villages, . . . will whisper confidentially in your ear: 'Ah! Sir, how unlike our thrifty Down East villages!'"[79] The wealth and hospitality evident on this unseen plantation responded to the curse's charge. In an inversion of Hundley's encounter, the *Delaware Gazette* finds that the memes of "sunny South" went unrealized on the ground. "The South," it claims, "has long appeared to the credulous eyes of the North as aristocratic, cultivated, and refined, with chivalric hosts and beautiful and accomplished women. That there are such to be found here and there is not disputed, but so far as the mass of the people are concerned, there was never a greater scam." "In everything that belongs to true civilization," the *Gazette* concludes, the South was surpassed by the Sandwich Islands.[80]

In 1854, a southern traveler remarks, somewhat unconvincingly, that "fashion draws us so strongly toward the watering places of the North, that we overlook the attractions of our own region of the country, . . . the amenities of Southern homes, and the kindness of Southern hospitality."[81] Among the amenities frequently found lacking in the South were adequate hotels. Responding to that charge as it appeared in the *New York Daily Times*, John R. Thompson of the *Southern Literary Messenger* concedes that "as a general rule Northern hotels are vastly better than Southern ones" but insists that in the South "no gentleman need ever stop at a tavern as a matter of necessary." "He may be an utter stranger," Thompson notes, "but he will not lack, on that account, a cordial invitation to some gentleman's mansion."[82] In *New England and Her Institutions*, Jacob Abbott responds to British charges of inferior American hotels by explaining that this was true only in the South. For Abbott, the squalor of southern taverns was clearly an effect of slavery, which incentivized the "slack and lazy" slave to servile "fidelity" only by means of "the lash." "A traveller in the south," he writes, "who sees slavery only as it appears to him in the taverns and along the highways, must be deeply impressed with the fact that it is a most serious political and social curse." Burdened with "a paralysis upon industry and improvement," Abbott concludes, "the southerners generally are not aware how far the northern states are in advance of them in intelligence and enterprise and power."[83]

Remarkably, though, Abbott adds to his "tribute of sympathy for the poor slave" a tribute to southern hospitality. Declaring his "admiration of the hospitality which adorns the southern character," Abbott reports that "a traveller with the garb and manners of gentleman finds a welcome at every door." Slipping into a pseudoiterative mode wherein the particular instance implies infinite replication, "He sees a plantation" —and the "gentleman of the house is already upon the steps." "Here, Thomas," the host commands, "Thomas, take this gentleman's horse. Walk in, sir; walk in. Thomas, take good care of the horse. Rub him down well, and give him as much grain as he will eat. I am very happy to see you, sir; walk in." As an adjunct to southern hospitality, Thomas, who can only be an enslaved person, ceases to be a slave. Conspicuously absent are the lash and squalor associated with slavery's curse. In a formulation that displaces the source of labor from the enslaved to the house, Abbott describes how as "you enter the house," the "best it affords is at your service." "At once," he continues, "you are at home"—at least if "you are a gentleman in manners and information."[84] Functionally, hospitality causes slavery to vanish and the plantation to appear, and at the same time it persuades Abbott to stop being a northerner and start being a gentleman. Little wonder, then, that abolitionist discourse strove to identify hospitality as an argument and to challenge the idea, as the *Southern Literary Journal* put it in 1837, that "in the Southern States" hospitality was "indigenous."[85]

As with southern hospitality, chivalric memes often translated an argument about slavery into a defense of a slaveholding people. Remnants of a feudal past, many of them borrowed from the novels of Walter Scott, proved of great interest when what was originally an argument over slavery between the United States and Britain became an argument between the North and the South. Again, there were two sides to the argument, as is evident in John L. Magee's famous 1856 lithograph of Preston Brooks caning Charles Sumner entitled "Southern Chivalry: Argument versus Club's."[86] More humorously, the mock-epic "Adventures of G. Whillikens, C.S.A" (1861) sung "of glorious Southern Chivalry; / of freedom based on slavery."[87] Referring to chivalry as "*the* chivalry" invariably signaled derision and scorn, as in "Song of the Pardon-Seekers," a poem published in 1866 in an African American newspaper located in Hampton, Virginia:

> We're coming up from Charleston too, and all along the shore
> The chivalry on bended knee your mercy do implore.
> A year ago, and even less, we thought your scalp to wave
> Above the soil where slave's [sic] should toil o'er Freedom's
>   bloody grave.[88]

Southerners were well aware that chivalry was in an argument. After the *Richmond Republican* complained that "Northern

SOUTHERN CHIVALRY — ARGUMENT versus CLUB'S.

John L. Magee, "Southern Chivalry--Argument versus Club's,"
lithograph (1856). Courtesy of the Boston Public Library, Digital
Commonwealth, Massachusetts Collections Online.

journalists laughed and rapped out stale jests about 'Quattle-
bums,' 'Southern Chivalry,' and all that," William Holden's
Weekly North Carolina Standard observed that the Richmond paper had itself employed "these 'flash' terms."[89] In *A
Defense of the South against the Reproaches and Incroachments of the North*, the Reverend Iveson Brookes claims that
the valor of southerners "entitled them to the epithet 'chivalric,' not in abolition sarcasm, but in the best, the true import
of the term."[90]

At a broader level, Brookes insists that "history must concede to the society of the slaveholding states, the traits of noble-
mindedness, kind-heartedness, benevolence, generosity, hospitality, politeness of manners, as characteristic of the citizens
of the south." But if the traits of a slaveholding people had
evolved to appear self-evident, they had done so within the
discursive context named in the title of his book and in support of the project identified in its subtitle: to reveal slavery
"as an institution God intended to form the basis of the best
social state."[91]

Minds and Bloods

As Jefferson predicted, angry and passionate iterations of the argument over slavery deepened the line marked by it. Although soft memes would be more likely to survive the war, they tended to harden, to mutate into more virulent forms, as the reproaches of the North grew louder. Group difference was more frequently expressed as group antagonism. As late as 1859, William Cabell Rives, who thought little of slavery and less of secession, could offer a conciliatory image of Virginia's enduring "Cavalier traits": "a genial fondness for sports and diversions, and elastic joyousness of temper, a free and uncalculating hospitality, and too great proneness to inaction and self-indulgence, except when the public cause summoned to exertion."[92] However, a more militant Cavalier had by this time gained ascendancy. Heat had long made the southern people leisurely and hospitable, but as the war approached, it was more likely, as Fitzhugh suggests, to make them energetic—one of the great slaveholding peoples of the world.

Heat increasingly affected not only habits but minds. Writing at the close of the war, John William Draper concludes that the cold caused the northern man to be industrious and reflective, while heat made the southern man indolent and impulsive. "A Southern nation," he writes, "which is continually under the influence of the sky, which is continually prompted to varying thoughts, will indulge in a superfluity of ideas, and deal with them all superficially." The northern mind, by contrast, is "cut off from the promptings of external nature," considers ideas "from many points of view," and is "apt to fasten itself intently on one, and pursue it with fantastical perseverance."[93] In *Uncle Tom's Cabin*, Augustine St. Clare, whose "characterological 'indolence,'" according to Jennifer Rae Greeson, is attributed in part to "climactic determinism," has a similar insight.[94] Avoiding serious talk and the thinking it involves during hot weather, St. Clare comes to understand "why northern nations are always more virtuous than southern ones."[95]

This idea, too, had a Dixie variant: namely, the idea, passionately held by southern intellectuals, that the South did not overvalue ideas. Shortly after the war, the *New Eclectic*, based in Baltimore, remarks that "our faults, shortcomings, vices if you will, have at least this redeeming feature, that they are natural," and thus free of Northern "isms"— that is, "what in New England are called 'ideas'—things which the healthy nature of our people loathes."[96] This recalls Fitzhugh's complaint in *Cannibals, All!* of the nefarious and "multitudinous isms of the North"—socialism, communism, abolitionism, millennialism, free love—that, due to the protections of slavery, were "unknown at the South." "Free Society every where," Fitzhugh insists, "begets isms, and . . . isms soon beget bloody revolutions."[97] In *Sociology for the South*, whose subtitle, "the failure of free society," captures its main argument, Fitzhugh argues that slavery was "a form, and the very best form, of socialism" and, to boot, "a beautiful example of communism, where each one receives not according to his labor, but according to his wants." Slavery was "the only practicable form of socialism" because it alone had been practiced; the revolutionaries of 1848 had theorized on air.[98] Karl Marx was not impressed, declaring the South to be a mere battle slogan and not a country at all.

Although Fitzhugh persuaded few that slavery was a form of socialism or communism, the idea that the institution had concrete, realized virtues had long served as a talking point. Of all the isms, abolitionism, which Fitzhugh claims "swallows up the little isms," required the most careful correction through practical, concrete demonstration.[99] In defending slavery as a positive good, Calhoun denies "having pronounced slavery in the abstract a good"; he refers instead "to existing circumstances; to slavery as a practical, not an abstract thing."[100] To Thomas Clarkson, an English abolitionist, John Henry Hammond writes, "If you were to ask me whether I was an advocate of slavery in the abstract, I should probably answer, that I am not. . . . I do not like to deal in abstractions; it seldom leads to any useful ends." "Our relations with one another, and with all matter," he insists, "are real, not ideal."[101] Writing to David M. Clarkson of New-burgh, New York, Edward Pollard suggests that his friend's concern with the "abstract cause of morality" was "unjust to the facts of the case." His own suffering had taught Pollard the foolishness of making "the abstract lots of men in this world an object of sympathy." He worried especially that the slave's "happiness" would be compromised "by the single abstract reflection that he lacks 'liberty' (*abolition liberty*, mark you)," scare quotes and italics marking phrases in dispute.[102] On the "abstract question of slavery" or "slavery, as an abstract question," southern perspectives differed, but a consensus emerged around the idea expressed by William Waters Boyce in the House of Representatives: namely, that the "anti-slavery feeling of the North" was "founded on some higher law than reason—a belief, a sentiment, a peremptory abstraction." "A conscientious belief," according to Boyce, "however erroneous, when it acquires entire possession of a single mind, absorbs every other feeling," and the northern mind, so infected, had focused its "abstract benevolence on the black race of the South."[103] Eventually this benevolence would seem racialized and predatory, as for J. Quitman Moore, who explains that the "natural antagonisms" between the Puritan (a "thinker and speculator") and Cavalier revealed themselves when the "idealism of the North encountered the realism of the South" as the North looked "to future political conquest and subjugation."[104] As with hospitality and its love of leisure, the South's "rage against abstraction," to borrow Fred Hobson's phrase, would survive the slavery controversy. And like those stipulated traits, it began there.[105]

Along with the peculiar institution came "the peculiar feelings of the South"—feelings "wantonly outraged," according to *De Bow's*, by the North's "settled spirit of hostility."[106] The southern mind, claims Virginia governor John B. Floyd in 1849, had coalesced against "the anti-slavery feeling of the North." For Floyd, "the almost unanimous sentiment of the slaveholding country" against abolitionist "fanati-

cism"—the word inevitably used—wasn't a matter of "political agitation" or "party prejudices" but an "almost unanimous sentiment of the slaveholding country"—indeed, the
"spontaneous outburst of a whole people." Placing the expression of a "whole people" beyond mere politics, Floyd uses
the idea of southern feeling, and thus the idea of the southern
people, as a weapon against what evolved as its most reliable
antagonist: an abstract conception of a fanatical North.[107]

So hypostatized, the mind of the North again transformed
an argument over slavery into a difference between peoples
that was as in the past confirmed by memes of climate and
blood. Inveighing against "assailants . . . united in all the es-
sentials of antagonism to slavery," William Lowndes Yancey
insists that the institution existed "for the benefit of the
South," and must, "in the hour of its peril, assailed by the
great Northern antagonistic force, . . . look to the South alone
for protection." But the difference ran deeper than political
antagonism. "The Creator," Yancey affirms,

> has beautified the face of this Union with sectional features.
> Absorbing all minor sub-divisions, He has made the North and
> the South; the one the region of frost, ribbed in with ice and
> granite; the other baring its generous bosom to the sun and ever
> smiling under its influence. The climate, soil and productions of
> these two grand divisions of the land, have made the character
> of their inhabitants. Those who occupy the one are cool, calcu-
> lating, enterprising, selfish, and grasping; the inhabitants of the
> other, are ardent, brave, and magnanimous, more disposed to
> give than to accumulate, to enjoy ease rather than to labor.[108]

Increasingly, as Ritchie Devon Watson has shown, the word
"race" was used designate the difference between South and
North.[109] "Anglo-Norman" supplanted "Anglo-Saxon" as
the preferred term of supposed genealogical inevitability. In
Sociology for the South, Fitzhugh assigns the "infidel Isms
at the North" to "Our Pilgrim fathers" who carried to the
northern colonies the fanaticism of Knox and Cromwell. In
the South, by contrast, a "love of personal liberty and freedom" had been inherited from "our Anglo-Saxon ances-

tors."[110] By 1861, however, Fitzhugh's South had been settled by "master races": "Cavaliers, Jacobites, and Huguenots"— races, he explains, who were "of Norman descent." "The Puritans who settled the North," on the other hand, were a "slave race" descended from the "Saxons and the Angles, [who] came from the cold and marshy regions of the North." Given this racial difference, Fitzhugh claims, it was a "gross mistake to suppose that abolition alone is the cause of dissention between North and South."[111] The leisurely habits of the Virginia Cavalier gave way to a sterner and more broadly diffused figure. As J. Quitman Moore explains, the "Cavalier, or Anglo-Norman element that had presided at the founding of the original Southern colonies"—all of them, apparently— had spread, "mingling the refinement of the courtier with the energy of the pioneer." Carrying "with them that same deep master-passion—an abiding attachment to landed possession and territorial power, which is the secret of the universal dominion and ascendancy of the Norman race," these new populations had "laid the foundations of a great, agricultural empire" and "gave to Southern civilization a character, racially different and distinct from that . . . of the Roundhead."[112]

The North and South, of course, had not become more (or less) Anglo-Saxon or Norman in the meantime, nor had English folkways erupted after a period of dormancy. But the memes had evolved and now marked a harder and more antagonistic boundary. While in 1851, *De Bow's* mocks Trescot's "discovery" that "the Ohio River and the Potomac, being such grand national barriers as must . . . constitute of necessity the nations on either side of them, diverse, independent, *hostile* to each other and capable of being at best but *'unequally* yoked together,'" a decade later it not only confirms Fitzhugh's genealogical explanation of inevitable hostility but offers its own slightly different account as well.[113] In the aftermath of Harper's Ferry, the magazine explains that "the immediate proximate cause of Northern hatred for the South is ENVY" because "we are happy in our society, and have slaves, denied to them by the coldness of their climate and sterility of their soil." But the deeper cause was "hereditary," such that "the attack on the institution of slavery is only a kind of adventitious opportunity eagerly caught up for this antagonism to develop itself." The antagonism ran to the Cavaliers and Puritans of seventeenth-century England, the Cavalier (in this instance) "being of the pure Anglo-Saxon blood" but sharing with his Norman cousin membership in "a gallant, high-spirited, chivalrous race." Opposite stood, predictably, the Puritan. "Misanthropy, hypocrisy, diseased philanthropy, envy, hatred, and all the worst passions of the human heart, were the ruling characteristics of the English puritans; and they continue to be the ruling characteristics of New England Yankees," their "lineal descendants." Little wonder, then, their "hatred and envy of all who may be their superiors by nature or circumstance."[114]

And yet it is doubtful that many southerners believed they constituted a distinct race or that they even had any clear notion of what a race was. As Michael O'Brien observes, "Southerners themselves did not always know what they meant by the word," which could be grounded in biology, ethnicity, ethnology, or biblical authority ("the Hametic race").[115] But then as now, when we also don't know what race is, it defined a harder group edge than did competing nomenclatures and generated more rage. But who comprised the southern race, however it was understood? This was a vexed question, since all agreed that the group excluded many persons living in the southern states, a bare majority of whom, O'Brien estimates, spoke English as a first language.[116] Most obviously excluded were persons of African descent, who were of a different race—either the race of Ham (as construed by the Bible) or the race of Blacks (as construed by contemporaneous science). One searches prewar discourse in vain for any reference to "the southern people" or "race"—any use of the term "southerner"—that conceivably includes people of color. Also troublesome were the multitudes of whites clearly not descended from Normans or even Anglo-Saxons: the Germans, Spanish, French, Irish, and Scots-Irish. Attempting to square the circle of southern blood, William Falconer explains in 1860 (as if for the first time) that southern blood was Norman blood, not the blood of Puritans "descended of the ancient Britons and Saxons." This "difference of race," Falconer insists, considered from a perspective "historical and philosophical, as contradistinguished from political," obliged "Southrons" to "rule the Northern people" lest they prove "false to the instincts of the NORMAN RACE." But, Falconer adds, "By the words southern people, is not meant all the people of the South, but that controlling element which . . . gives character to the whole." This was the "*representative* blood of the South"—not all of it, perhaps, but that flowing through the veins of "the *Southern* people in the main."[117]

A difference between the *southern* people and the people of the Southeast could also be identified on the basis of economic class. Only a small fraction of whites living in the region legally owned slaves and a minority lived in slave-owning households. And yet as abolitionist George M. Weston notes in his 1856 book *The Poor Whites of the South*, he does not "recollect ever to have seen or heard these non-slaveholding whites referred to by Southern gentlemen, as constituting any part of what they call '*the South*.'"[118] Identifying "the South" as a construct of slaveholding persons, not the inevitable outcome of a slaveholding people, Weston proved useful to Hinton Rowan Helper, who, in *The Impending Crisis* (1857), quotes him approvingly, adding additional scare quotes around the word "gentleman." For Helper, nothing about "*the South*" was inevitable or self-evident, including its "gentlemen" and the purported relation of climate and slavery. Noting that there is no "degree of latitude" anywhere in the United States where "the rays of sun become too calorific for white men," he observes that "in the South we find a very large number of non-slaveholding whites over the age of fifteen, who derive their entire support from manual labor in the open fields." The sun, he concludes, is a "bugbear of slaveholding demagogues."[119]

But unlike Weston, Helper was, in his words, a "Southerner by instinct and by all the influences of thought, habits, and kindred"—a man who planned to live and die "within the limits of the South." Even so, he declares that the "the first and most sacred duty of every Southerner . . . is to declare himself an uncompromising abolitionist," and he wields abolitionist memes with uncompromising vigor. "Proof upon proof" showed slavery to be "an oppressive burden to the blacks, and an incalculable injury to the whites," this injury compelling him the most. Efforts to "turn the curse of slavery into a blessing" were "amazing to credulity, and insulting to intelligence"; statistic after statistic proved that the South had lagged economically. Poor whites, "made poor and ignorant by the system of slavery," were the especial victims, consigned to poverty, illiteracy, and social disgrace.[120] And yet the slave "oligarchs" (a term Helper uses nine times) or "oligarchy" (which he uses thirty times) had hoodwinked the masses into believing that slavery was a foundational "institution." To the word "institution," which references a foundational inevitability, he attaches colorful adjectives locating it in an argument; among these are "ungodly," "unprofitable," "diabolical," "accursed," "degrading," "pernicious," "damnable," "vile," "baneful," "iniquitous, "pagan," "inhuman," and "wicked."[121] To "lords of the lash," an already prevalent abolitionist meme, he adds mocking variants: "Messieurs lords of the lash," "august knight[s] of the whip and the lash."[122] But however colorful his rhetoric, Helper conspicuously failed to deconstruct a slaveholding people. Having "indulged the hope" (surely rhetorical) that his book would be received by his "fellow-Southrons" in "a reasonable and friendly spirit," he found, as a practical matter, his claim to southernness disqualified.[123] Declared a traitor and heretic, he fled the wrath of the southern people, and possession of his book was declared, in several states, a capital offense.

The fate of the "hated Helper," as he came to be known, not only speaks to the "almost unanimous sentiment of the slaveholding country" but also shows how deeply the memes of a slaveholding people had taken hold. Increasingly, "the people," as George Washington Cable would later observe, constituted only "that part of the population which allowed . . . itself to be so called."[124] And this was true despite—or, more likely, because of—increasingly extravagant efforts to write a people *as if writing from a people*. The figure of Cavalier, as Singal argues, provided no middle ground for southerners who deviated from type and thus excluded most people living in the Southeast.[125] Greeks, Romans, Normans, feudal lords, or medieval knights, all of whom were used, in one way or another, to mark and extend the prehistory of the southern people did not live in the south (although some number of royalists had settled there). These figures rendered grander and more inevitable what was, as Lewis Simpson observes, "the most novel part of the novel nation in history," a chattel slave society without "historical reference in the Anglo-Saxon civilization from which its religion, law, and letters descended" and lacking "any very credible parallels in contemporary slave societies."[126] What Fred Hobson calls the southern "rage to explain" devolved, as the war approached, into less explanation and more rage, which lent to these figures, in Barthes's words, a "clarity which is not that of an explanation but that of a statement of fact."[127] It became obvious who a southerner was; no explanation was needed.

The North, too, assembled around notions no less fantastical. Among these was a favorite of Helper's: the slave power. "It is madness," he insists, for "non-slaveholding whites of the South" to "suppose that they will ever be able to rise to a position of true manhood, until after the slave power shall have been utterly overthrown."[128] The idea of *the* slave power—the article hypostatizing it—spread virally during the 1850s and, contra Helper's intention, helped to transform an argument about slavery into an antagonism between North and South. In its most neutral form, the term referred to the disproportionate power held by slaveholders in national affairs. But the idea came to conjure a mysterious cabal bent on forcing the institution on the entire nation and continent.[129] At times little more than a conspiracy theory, the idea of the slave power was effective in forming alliances between abolitionists and white farmers and workers, many of them unconcerned with the plight of the enslaved. As Jennifer Rae Greeson shows, Garrison's *Liberator* had increasingly detached its "crusade for abolition of slavery from any implicit critique of the relative freedom of 'free labor' under northeastern industrialization," anchoring it instead in "lurid depictions of depraved and sinful planter lusts." "In perpetual ideological flight from . . . comparative materialist analysis of slave capitalism and industrial capitalism," she remarks, "Garrisonian writers made 'work or starve' appear a humanitarian proposition."[130] By contrast, the slave power potentially spoke to the concerns of the working class by aligning the malevolent oligarchies of southern planters and northern industrialists. The "lord of the lash" often appeared alongside the "lords of the loom," while the *Anti-Slavery Bugle* proclaimed that "the Wealth of the North and the Wealth of the South are combined to crush the liberal, free, progressive spirit of the age."[131]

The slave power repeated in a different way two points southern spokesmen had long made: that the southerner was born to rule and that the world's industrial economy rested on the South's agricultural empire. To a correspondent who spoke "sneeringly of 'the slave power,'" Brookes responds that he "should as well call southern influence by its proper name, intellectual power."[132] The economic question could be addressed in the spirit of sectional cooperation. Senator Joseph R. Underwood of Kentucky affirmed that he did "not believe there is a particle of truth in the idea of conflicting interests, growing out of slave power. On the contrary, I think it can be demonstrated that the manufacturing, navigating, and commercial interest of the free States are eminently advanced by the tobacco, cotton, rice, and sugar interests of the South, and *vice versa*."[133]

But it could also be addressed with the utmost antagonism, most famously in Hammond's mudsill speech of 1858. On the Senate floor, Hammond confirmed Senator William

Seward's "complain[t] of the rule of the South" by declaring that "cotton is king." Not only had the South's "great career of enterprise" made the world's economy dependent on it but "the slaveholders of the South" had built the country. Unlike the North, the South enjoyed a "harmony of her political and social institutions . . . such that no other people ever enjoyed upon the face of the earth." "All social systems," Hammond claims, require a "class to do the menial duties, to perform the drudgery of life"—the "very mud-sill of society"—so that the "other class which leads progress, civilization, and refinement" can exist. For its mudsill, the South had found a "race inferior to its own, but eminently qualified in temper, in vigor, in docility, in capacity to stand the climate, to answer all her purposes." Compared with "your whole hireling class of laborers," enslaved persons were "hired for life and well compensated," materially comfortable and devoid of revolutionary aspirations. That enslaved persons were better off than Northern laborers had been claimed hundreds of times; that they, unlike those workers, did not threaten the social order had been claimed dozens. What Hammond added was the claim that laborers were "effectively slaves." "Our slaves are black," he proclaims. "Yours are white, of your own race; you are brothers of one blood."[134]

In his *History of the Rise and Fall of the Slave Power* (1874), Henry Wilson asserts that Hammond's "open avowal" of what other southerners believed but "did not deem . . . politic to express" "opened the eyes of men to the spirit, aims, and purposes of the Slave Power as perhaps no previous demonstration had been able to effect."[135] "Hammond's object," reports the *Raftman's Journal* of Clearfield, Pennsylvania, "is to degrade free white labor and reduce it to the level with the negro slave labor of the south." "What workingman can read this insulting language and not feel his blood boil in his veins?"[136] The *Nevada Democrat*, distant from the fray and close to the Democratic Party, objects to Hammond's equation of white laborers with "the rough timber on which well polished, aristocratic boots may tread above the polluting dirt of the labor-field."[137] As Michael E. Woods has shown, "mudsill" was adopted as a term of pride by numerous "Mud-Sill Clubs" throughout the Northeast, later appearing regularly in the songs and letters of Union soldiers, often juxtaposed against an enemy called "the chivalry."[138] Shortly after the outbreak of the Civil War, for example, the *New York Daily Tribune* ran an enlistment ad announcing that the "so-called SOUTHERN CHIVALRY, in their attempt to degrade HONEST LABOR, would place the NORTHERN MECHANIC on the same grade as the Southern slave. They call us NORTHERN MUD-SILLS and GREASY MECHANICS. Shall we submit to SOUTHERN REBELS and enslave our children?"[139]

Despite its theoretical potential to assemble groups along lines of labor and capital, the slave power instead reinscribed boundaries of section and race. Hammond's specific insult had come from a planter; eventually it would seem to come from a South that held the laborer in contempt. According to Leonard L. Richards, "hostility toward slave oligarchs . . . provided common ground" for northern whites who might "differ on scores of issues, hate blacks or like them, denounce slavery as a sin or guarantee its protection in the Deep South."[140] And if, as Larry Gara argues, the Republican Party hoped "to appeal to non-slaveholders in the South as well as to northern voters if they presented the question properly as 'a question of the white man against the Ethiopian,'" the looming threat of "Black Republicanism" quashed the hope.[141] One explanation for why the slave power flourished in the North and languished in the South is that slavery threatened to turn white men into slaves in the North but made it impossible for white men in the South to be slaves. Trescot extends the idea: to the commonplace that slavery had elevated "all citizens" of South Carolina "to a condition of a privileged class," he adds that as a result, "the whole South became slaveholders."[142]

The appeal of this idea partially explains the willingness of nonslaveholders to count themselves among a slaveholding people, but it meant that for writers like Hammond, there could be no poor whites in the South. They might, however, exist in South Carolina, whose governor (Hammond, as it turns out) had, eight years earlier, complained that poor whites "obtain a precarious existence by occasional jobs, by hunting, by fishing, by plundering fields or folds, and often by what is in its effects far worse—trading with slaves, and seducing them to plunder for their benefit."[143] But because they could not be counted among a slaveholding people, they were consigned to what Falconer calls that part of "the population of the Southern States which does not come of *the true normal race*, and are, therefore destitute of those [controlling] characteristics."[144] In this view, the true normal race comprised southerners; poor whites merely lived in the vicinity. For abolitionists, conversely, poor whites inhabited not just the southern states, but the South, where they functioned as a powerful indictment of the peculiar institution. In her *Key to Uncle Tom's Cabin*, Stowe makes note of the South's "common reply" to European indignation over slavery—namely, "look at your own lower classes." But Stowe enjoins southerners to consider their own. Slavery had produced not only "heathenish, degraded, miserable slaves" but also "poor white trash," a "class of white people who are, by universal admission, more heathenish, degraded, and miserable."[145] Olmsted's *Cotton Kingdom*—its title a clear jab at Hammond—reveals a white populace consigned by slavery to a life of "bare necessities"—"poor shelter, poor clothing, and the crudest diet"—and "immeasurably poorer than the mass of the people in the adjoining Free States."[146] Whether a talking point or a figure generating conspicuous silence, the poor white was usually embedded in the argument over slavery.

A more complex response came from Hundley, who concedes the existence of the "poor white trash" but claims that the group was no fault of slavery. These folk, he maintains, were naturally lazy, reasonably comfortable, and relatively content to live in the hills. It was the "honey-tongued libellers," the "accusers of the South," who insisted on the tripartite division of "Cavaliers, Poor Whites, and Slaves." For Hundley, a Unionist, the southern states comprised a diversity of types, many of them straddling sectional boundaries. The planter might be a southern gentleman (who actually *had* descended, at least "chiefly," from English Cavaliers and French Huguenots), a cotton snob (the kind of uncouth pretender who jousted), or, worst of all, a southern Yankee given to laying on the lash in his "tireless pursuit of riches." But there were also the southern middle classes, which "constitute[d] the greater proportion of . . . citizens"; the southern yeoman, who was as different from the poor whites as the southern gentleman was from the cotton snob, and the southern bully, a tobacco-chewing drunk "cocked and primed, in his own vernacular—to flog the entire North." In presenting a heterogeneous picture of the southern states, Hundley hoped to prevent a "Quixotic war" like the one waged by "the foolish one-idead knights of the old days of chivalry." To this end, he would not repeat the mistake of the London bookseller who, in Hundley's cautionary tale, did good business by "*always let[ing] the vulgar correct me; whenever popular clamor arises I always echo the million . . . . thus every man buys the book, not to learn new sentiments, but to have the pleasure of seeing his own reflected.*"[147]

But for all his conciliatory intent, Hundley echoed the million in defending the peculiar institution. The disagreement over slavery was too deep to be resolved by efforts that minimized differences between South and the North. Hundley's chapter titled "Poor White Trash," for example, is devoted less to its subject than the abolitionist abuse of the figure. From a heated denunciation of "the windy fanaticism and overhot zeal" of both Fire Eaters and Black Republicans, he returns to the poor white momentarily, only to swerve again to denounce the demagogues of New England, who "may rant about social equality" but "know in their hearts that such a thing is simply an impossible abstraction."[148] Six times Hundley begins his paragraph "but to return," all after being carried away from his subject by a compulsion to inveigh against "abolition fanaticism." Given the premise of his book, he rarely uses the term "southerner" to describe a kind of person, except as the kind of person slandered for his association with slavery. "Abolition parsons," he complains, "have been praying so devoutly for God to heap coals of fire upon the heads of the Southerners."[149] And so, even as Hundley subdivides the South into "the Southern states" and a single people into a diverse populace, he draws on the same affective substrate—rage against northern representations of the slaveholding South—more powerfully mobilized by simpler memes. Relative to the uninspiring southern yeoman and southern middle classes, the Cavalier and Norman, both destined to rule the Yankee race, proved more compelling. Clamorously echoed by the million, they more clearly marked friend and enemy, to borrow Carl Schmitt's classic formulation, and heightened the intensity of association and dissociation.

Hence the success of Page's "few phrases about 'cavaliers' and 'great planters'" that had come to "make a picture in the public mind"—enough of one, at any rate, to assemble an army and a navy to wage war against "those people over there." But the few phrases of Page's own time did not form the formless associations defining the South in the same way they had done in antebellum period. They were phrases from the past carried forward in the form of Confederate ghosts, and the plantation they referenced no longer existed. And yet the memes of a slaveholding people would replicate even in the absence of the peculiar institution.

CHAPTER 2

The South under Reconstruction

That the southern people were, as William Henry Trescot insists, "indebted to the institution of slavery . . . for all that we are" was a common sentiment among southerners. And so it is little wonder that in 1866 we find Edward Pollard fretting that a defeated South might "lose its moral and intellectual distinctiveness as a people." "Slavery," he claims, had "established in the South a peculiar and noble type of civilization," a civilization he traces to "the Cavaliers who sought the brighter climes of the South." Defeat at the hands of the "modern *Yankee*," descended from "Puritan exiles who established themselves upon the rugged and cheerless soil of New England," meant that the South, like a defeated Greece, might "experience the extinction of [its] literature, the decay of mind, and the loss of [its] distinctive forms of thought." To prevent this extinction, Pollard calls for a "war of ideas" that might perpetuate the southerners' "polite manners, their fine sentiments, their attachment to a sort of feudal life, their landed gentry," ideas to which he adds one that stuck: "the lost cause," which was the title of his book. For Pollard, chivalry partially explained why the cause had been lost. Having long "worshipped the grosses types of physical power," the northern people had "exhibited gross materialism in this war," while the "exhibitions of generalship, chivalry, humanity and all that noble sentimentalism that properly belongs to the state of war have been more largely on the Confederate side." The "Southern people were so proud of their reputation for chivalry," he insists, that, despite "enemy's barbarities," they "were willing to sacrifice for it almost any other passion of the war." This was a decided disadvantage against the likes of Sherman, who, despite being a "mediocre and insignificant" tactician, "essayed a new code of cruelty in war."[1]

Although its importance would diminish, chivalry, then, survived in the war of ideas distinguishing the peoples of the North and South. But it functioned differently after the war. It had to. Before, it had explained why the southern people would triumph over the craven Yankee race; after, it would explain their defeat by a barbarous and industrialized people. Since it could no longer be attached to slavery's feudal order, Pollard worried whether the South's "well-known superiourity in civilization" would survive.[2] But perhaps he also feared that a man such as Benjamin H. Hill, a Confederate general remembered for "his large heart, which ever beat in true Southern chivalry," would have different ideas. In an 1871 address delivered in Athens, Georgia, Hill insists that "far more than in any other age, ideas govern mankind." "Thought" being the "Hercules of this age," Hill hopes that it might "clea[n] out the Augean stables of accumulated social errors," among which he ranks foremost the institution of slavery. The "earth contain[ing] no white race superior to the Southern people," a people blessed with the "most fertile" of soils and the "most genial" of climates, the South had been "most deleteriously affected" by the institution. As planters enjoyed dissipated lives of "elegant leisure, luxurious abandon, and hospitable idleness," the South had lagged, "especially in *material* and commercial development."[3] This southern variant of the curse-of-slavery thesis replicated much more successfully than Hinton Rowan Helper's iteration before the war, when cotton had been king, not cumbrance.

In exploring the evolution of the notional South in the aftermath of the war, it is best to acknowledge up front that the process was uneven and uncertain. The memes of Dixie continued to respond to northern countermemes, assembling different groups of southerners according to different logics. However, they were always detached from the peculiar institution of slavery, despite the fact that it had often seemed to be their foundation. The curse of slavery lingered, both as moral accusation and economic burden, but even with slavery gone (and good riddance!) the blessings it had bestowed—hospitality, traditionalism, localism, a slower pace of life—would continue to characterize the southern people. They, in turn, were less often *a people* and more often "southerners," who, although they continued to differ from "northerners," were part of the same nation-state, the war having settled, irrevocably, the question of a separate national existence. As memes evolved, they continued to serve as flags to rally around, although without risking the possibility of adjacent artillery. Eventually, a southern way of life would emerge that would give rise to a new social order as organic and inevitable as slavery had been. But the transformation of history into nature occurred in fits and starts, and it was not clear within the welter of the times which South would survive to appear timeless.

No one illustrates the point better than Pollard himself, who, as I've argued elsewhere, toggled from South to South with little regard for consistency.[4] Having sneered in 1866 at the "clattering and garish enterprise of the North," he actively courted it his 1870 *The Virginia Tourist*. Shifting the object of his veneration from Old South to New, Pollard reveals that the lost cause had an upside: the "discovery of Virginia and the Southern States by the Yankees," who, finding "new kingdoms of commerce and industry," would bring to the South enterprise, capital, "better management," and the "art of advertising." These would repair the harms caused by the "past system of slavery."[5]

In the interim, Pollard imagined two additional Souths,

both posited as inevitabilities, both responding to the contingencies of the moment. The South of *The Lost Cause Regained* (1868) was no longer a separate civilization but an integral part of a Union "peculiarly glorious and sacred." Pollard bases the "homogeneousness and identity of the nation" in this instance on "the supremacy of the white race," which stood threatened by Radical Republicanism and "the incubus of Negro rule." In this contest, Pollard insists, "the true cause of the war," as retroactively defined, might result in the lost cause being regained.[6] But having gone on at length about the impossibility of Black citizenship, Pollard reverses course two years later, announcing in "The Negro in the South" that his "former views of the negro were wrong." The "evidence of my own eyes" had shown Pollard that "black man promises to become a true follower of the highest civilization . . . and an exemplary citizen of the South." Chivalry, which had marked the South's superior civilization in *The Lost Cause*, would now form a paternalistic bond between the white man and the freedman he sought to champion: "The opportunity is to build up a true school of chivalry in the South founded on the black man—one of ingenuous and brave spirits; and to indicate in the cause of the rights and progress of the colored people of the South an honorable and romantic championship, raised far above the strife of mere political parties, and exalted to a great and knightly cause and contest in the affairs of this century." So conceived, chivalry would reinscribe the boundary between North and South by persuading "the colored people of the South" to abandon their "false friendships with the North" and align with the Democratic party.[7] This was a novel and altogether unsuccessful deployment of the chivalry meme. The political alliance failed to materialize, and in time chivalry would underwrite new projects of white supremacy—most notoriously, the second Ku Klux Klan.[8]

More typical of chivalry's role in defining the postwar South was an exchange between Albert Taylor Bledsoe and John William De Forest, a Union soldier best known as the author of *Miss Ravenel's Conversion from Secession to Loyalty* (1867). In two 1869 articles on "Chivalrous and Semi-Chivalrous Southrons," De Forest claims that "these 'Southrons'" were, indeed, "a different people from us Northerners"—as different, perhaps, "as the Spartans to the Athenians, or the Poles to the Germans." Conceding the southron's "provincial," "antique" and "picturesque" virtues, De Forest smilingly adds that he "is great in his own eyes not only because he is what he is, but because he lives where he lives. In these modern times there is no other civilized creature so local, and, if I may be offensive, so provincial, in sentiments, opinions, prejudices, and vanities, as he." The southron might offer a bow with the understanding that "no such delicate behavior was known among the Vandals north Mason and Dixon's line" and that "it could not easily be matched in Europe except among the loftiest nobility."[9] Only in the South would a "leading statesman" (Alexander Stephens) "write a ponderous political work in dialogue, after the fashion of the essays of Plato and Cicero," a "gusto of classical imitation" that "might possibly be found in a Harvard Sophomore." (A senior would know better.) Hopefully a "true Southern novelist" (not the sort who "tal[k] of themselves only in a spirit of self-adulation") would appear to depict realistically the "chivalrous Southron'"—and soon, for in a generation he would "be as dead as the slavery that created him."[10]

Responding to De Forest in the *Southern Review*, Bledsoe characterizes his depiction as part of a "continual stream of disparagement, ridicule, and falsehood" flowing forth from the northern press, the Freedman's Bureau, and the "negro Legislatures in the South" whose collective goal was "the alteration and extinction of the characteristics of the Southern people." Of the origin of "the difference in character . . . between the North and the South" Bledsoe was unsure: possibly it involved climate or "peculiar stocks of population"; probably slavery was insignificant. He was certain, however, that the question was "of very subordinate consequence." What mattered was that the "character of the 'chivalrous Southron' is the character of the South" and would continue to be, since "the character of nations," "once built up . . . , appears almost indestructible." For Bledsoe, "no conquered people will sink with their characteristics into the characteristics of their conquerors," especially a Yankee civilization wracked by "wretched materialism." The "chivalrous Southron" had always ruled and would again, despite the "infernal policy of making the negro the equal and ruler of the white race," which had disrupted the deep "sympathy between the white and black races" that had existed before emancipation. The cause of the late war was not, as "the Northerns say," slavery, but the mind of a North consumed with "hate" and "jealousy": "Therefore—'down with slavery! down with the South!' and having conquered the Southern people, now let their hated characteristics go out with slavery; laugh at them; ridicule them; crush them by negro association and negro rule, and make them imitate us, their lords and masters.' This is the policy."[11] Pollard sounds a similar note in *The Lost Cause*, explaining that the North "naturally found or imagined in slavery the leading cause of the distinctive [and superior] civilization of the South," and therefore "revenged itself on the cause, diverted its envy in an attack upon slavery, and defamed the institution as the relic of barbarism."[12]

But for Pollard, as we've seen, "negro rule" meant, in *The Lost Cause Regained*, abandoning the two civilizations thesis to assemble a unified white nation, yielding two final Souths, one that embraced the "wretched materialism" that Bledsoe found truly wretched and another that deployed "chivalry" as a paternalistic solution to "negro rule." What remained constant in all but the sunniest of the New Souths was the idea of a South under threat. Whether the threat was assimilation, materialism, poverty, or "negro rule," successful memes refashioned stigmata that could no longer be framed in terms of a competition but rather could only be understood in the context of loss. In losing the war, however, the South won Pollard's war of ideas. We still have ideas about it, many of them surviving "the experience of defeat" or constructed from that experience.

The War as Meme

As the war evolved memically, it became many things to many groups. What most often for the Confederacy had been termed the "War for Southern Independence" acquired multiple names that framed the conflict and its causes in different ways. The "War for Southern Independence" quickly lost its luster as a designation, likely because it reminded people that the project had failed. Pollard's *Lost Cause* refers to the "War of the Confederates," a contest between "two nations of opposite civilization" and by no means "a *'Southern Rebellion.'*" "Names are apparently slight things," he notes, "but they create the first impression" and "solicit the sympathies of the vulgar"; his record would "supply the proper definitions of the words we have referred to as falsely applied to the South."[13] Yet in *The Lost Cause Regained* Pollard describes the war as a "rebellion" against the Union, echoing northern terms ("the War of the Rebellion" or, more pointedly, "the Slaveholder's Rebellion") but reimagining the war as a win, since, in leading the cause of white supremacy, "the South is far stronger than in any former contest."[14] By the time of *The Virginia Tourist*, Pollard had settled on the "Civil War," a relatively neutral term that supported his effort to attract northern capital. Alexander Stephens, who had insisted that the Confederacy rested on the cornerstone of slavery, revised his view to propose a "War between the States." In this war, slavery (or "Slavery, so-called, because there was with us no such thing as Slavery in the full and proper sense of that word") was "of infinitely less importance to the Seceding States, than the recognition of this great principle": the "cause of Constitutional Liberty everywhere." In his two-volume "gusto of classical imitation," he characterizes the war a constitutional action taken on behalf of the "Federative principle of Government, against the principle of Empire!," which involved, even less plausibly, defending "the Grecian type of Civilization against the Asiatic."[15] Although the term "War of Northern Aggression" wouldn't appear until the civil rights era, its structure of feeling was predicted by Bledsoe's war of northern jealousy and Pollard's (initial) war of northern envy, both of which posited an invading horde threatening the homes and localities of the southern people. In this effort, the endangered fireside (or hearthstone) emerged as a touchstone. Today, the National Park Service website for Appomattox Court House claims that "a crucial motivator for many Southern soldiers was the defense of home and family against the invading Northern armies." Three of five quotations in support of that proposition mention firesides, the most colorful coming from Corporal George Knox Miller: "When a Southron's home is threatened, the spirit of resistance is irrepressible. [We are] fighting for our firesides and property [to defend our homes from] vandal enemies and drive them from the soil polluted by their footsteps."[16]

Perhaps the most powerful meme was the lost cause itself, a "nebulous condensation" that, like more clearly articulated causes, powerfully *dissociated* the war from any effort to establish a slaveholding republic. As W. J. Cash shrewdly observes, no Confederate soldier "ever died for anything so crass and unbeautiful as the preservation of slavery."[17] A war on behalf of southern civilization or to establish southern independence could be separated from cause of slavery per se, as could a war fought for the "cause of Constitutional Liberty everywhere" or against an envious and brutal invader. But the lost cause spoke to a larger, more sacralized effort, rendering, in its expansive imprecision, loss itself causal. Significantly, Pollard uses the term only in the title of his work. Over time, this conceptual impoverishment lent the meme a kind of affective stickiness, allowing it to accumulate manifold associations, most of which speak to the idea of an indi-

visible South. Of the hundred phrases "burned" into southern brains by the war, Cash says, "the key was in every case
the adjective Southern."[18] *The South*, and not Charleston or
Arkansas, had been defeated, although the group so assembled continued to exclude those in the Southeast who had
not lost the war.

Further, the lost cause marked what Thomas Dixon
would later call a "landmark of time": "Henceforth all
events would be reckoned from this; 'before the Surrender,'
or 'after the Surrender.'"[19] In *History in Transit*, Dominick
LaCapra writes that "every group that is in some significant sense a locus of commitment whose members affirm
(and may be pressured to affirm) a collective identity has
in its past or in its mythology (often its mythologized past)
a trauma that has become foundational and is a source of
identity both for those who actually lived through it and
in different ways for those born into its aftermath. In perhaps its most politically pointed dimensions, the founding
trauma may be way for a group . . . to reclaim a history and
to transform it into a more or less enabling basis of life in
the present."[20] For Robert Penn Warren, the war functioned
in precisely this way, giving "the South the Great Alibi" by
which "it "explains, condones, and transmutes everything."
"By a simple reference to the 'War,'" he claims, "any Southern female could, not too long ago, put on the glass slip-
per and be whisked away to a ball."[21] For William Faulkner, every fourteen-year-old southern boy compulsively
rehearsed Pickett's Charge and thought "this time. Maybe
this time."[22] At the broadest level, the war transformed, in
LaCapra's terms, lack into loss: it wasn't that the southern
family lacked silver but that the Yankees had stolen it. As
Jon Smith acutely observes in his Lacanian analysis of the
missing silver, "*The spoons are never coming back, so the
spoons are always present.*"[23]

But as a founding trauma, the war's foundation was
shifty, its loss never quite the same. It might assemble southerners around a developing fantasy of what the Old South

had been, or around a pantheon of Confederate heroes whose curated virtues exhibited facets of the southern character. But it might also figure, as for Hill and other progressives, as a kind of fortunate fall. Dixon offers a case in point, positioning loss as necessary for the "Old South," which "fought against the stars in their courses—the resistless tide of the rising consciousness of Nationality and World-Mission," to give way to the "young South," which "greets the new era and glories in its manhood," joining "his voice in the cheers of triumph which are ushering in this all-conquering Saxon!"[24]

Although exceptionally histrionic, Dixon's view was common among New South advocates. In his 1886 "New South" address, Henry Grady pronounces himself "glad that the omniscient God held the balance of the battle in His Almighty hand and that human slavery was swept forever from American soil—that the American Union was saved from the wreck of war." Finding "his social system, feudal in its magnificence, swept away," Grady's defeated Confederate soldier settles down to work with "cheerfulness and frankness," taking practical measures that herald a new day free of slavery's economic encumbrance.[25] With respect to the war specifically but also to the South more broadly, progressives generally worked with weaker memes. A war that was simply over, having settled questions of nationality and slavery, lacked the affective power of the lost cause, and New South boosterism always carried the taint of Yankee materialism. For Grady, the Revolutionary War, not the Civil one, had eliminated any differences between Cavalier and Yankee, and breaking up one plantation to allow for the creation of one hundred farms meant the right and proper diffusion of what once was "gathered in the hands of a splendid and chivalric oligarchy."[26] Grady might announce an intention to "carry the transcending traditions of the old South . . . unstained and unbroken into the new," but his heart was not in it.[27] Henry Watterson, meanwhile, famously pronounces the South to be merely a "geographical expression."[28] For his part, Dixon effectively buries the virtues of Old South in praising them: "old-fashioned, mediaeval, provincial, worshiping the dead, . . . tradition ridden" as well as "bombastic, romantic, chivalrous, lustful, proud, kind and hospitable." Dreams of "local supremacy," for Dixon, had happily given way to the "conquest of the globe" rendered possible by "annihilated time and space."[29]

Pollard, Hill, and many others had come to similar conclusions in the early years after the war, leading Allen Tate to complain that surrender marked an exile from the feudal Eden of the antebellum era, "though," he adds pointedly, "much less than the Irish have we ever been beaten in war."[30] For Tate, this marked another moment of paradox for a South that had begun as a capitalist enterprise at Jamestown, become feudal for a period, and then, lacking a proper religion, converted to the gospel of progress. His war, then, differs from Dixon's in two ways: first, the consequences of defeat are not inevitable (since the South could have remained southern, as the Irish remained Irish), and second, the imperative was for the South to remain feudal and agrarian, not, as for Dixon, to become modern and industrial. Tate's paradox, then, identifies a South that is fully wired to the politics and economics of the nation-state but that retains, despite the abnegation of its distinctive genius, its special character as what Cash calls "not a nation within a nation, but the next thing to it."[31]

In preventing the South from becoming a geographical expression, the postwar memes of Dixie largely operated within a melancholic logic that, according to Slavoj Žižek, reconciles groups to capitalist modernization by insisting "they should not renounce their tradition through mourning, but retain the melancholic attachment to their lost roots."[32] Drained of political meaning, the war could appear as the collective effort of a people whose distinctive traits were recognizable in it. As Richard Gray has shown, Confederate generals were fashioned into a kind of pantheon, each illustrating "some particular facet of the aristocratic model" so that "together, the Confederate high command formed a kind of tableau, a detailed and comprehensive portrait of 'the ancient chivalry' of the region and all its equally glamourous, uniformly flattering possibilities."[33] The exception was Robert E. Lee, whose indivisible perfection subsumed all facets. Lee's ambivalent views of slavery eventually morphed into something close to abolitionism. According to Allen Tate, Lee "never owned a slave and detested slavery," fighting instead "for the local community which he could not abstract into fragments."[34] The deification of Lee further detached causality from the lost cause, and he contributed to it through his reconciliationist stance after the war. In 1869, he refused an invitation to Gettysburg, pronouncing it "wiser . . . not to keep open the sores of war but to follow the examples of those nations who endeavored to obliterate the marks of civil strife, to commit to oblivion the feelings it engendered."[35] His wish, however, lacked the force of command, and his wisdom proved no match for the feelings engendered by, among others, Henry Timrod, whose Magnolia Cemetery Ode enjoins the "martyrs of a fallen cause" to sleep, "though yet no marble column craves / The pilgrim here to pause."[36] The marble would appear in time, including a recumbent statue of Lee funded, after his death, by sales of a lithograph commissioned by the Lee Memorial Association. The statue was installed at Lee's tomb on the campus of Washington and Lee University, a site that in time would become known as the Shrine of the South.

Vacated of historical and political specificity, Lee replicated with astonishing success and in direct opposition to the wishes of its referent. Upon the death of the "rebel chief," Frederick Douglass complained that southern papers were "filled with nauseating flatteries of the late ROBERT E. LEE; and many northern journals also join in these undeserved tributes to his memory."[37] According to the Philadelphia *Evening Telegraph*, the news of Lee's death "was received with regret throughout the country, and our exchanges generally from the North, as well as the South, without distinction of party, have kindly articles, in which much is said of the purity and dignity of his character."[38] Months later, a life-size lithograph of the Confederate general was featured among the "elegant appointments" of a Cairo, Illinois, restaurant.[39] But if Lee was admired north of the Mason-Dixon, south of it he was nearly worshiped. "Saint Robert," as Michael Fellman argues, filled a "continuously urgent need," serving as a "shining exemplar of all that was caring and pure and Christian."[40] There was a Union antipode, since, as Cash acutely observes, Sherman and Ben Butler joined Darwin and Satan in coming to "figure in Southern feeling as very nearly a single person."[41]

The idiom of martyrdom, pilgrimage, and sainthood marked the holiness of the Confederate cause, which was fully evident in General Jubal Early's 1872 oration at Lee's tomb. Within the space of two paragraphs, Early invokes the "holy cause" of the Confederacy, the "holy memories" of its "glorious though unsuccessful struggle," and the "sacred duty" incumbent on his audience: namely, to reproduce Lee yet again in a "monument to his glorious memory . . . at the Confederate Capital." Early's "fair countrywomen" would aid in the work of replication, continuing to "honor the brave dead" by "strew[ing] flowers on their graves," thereby instilling "the sentiments of honor and patriotism into the hearts of the rising and future generations." [42] In his invocation to replicate, Early exemplifies how, as Eric Santner argues, the compulsive, iterative aspect of "covenantal enjoinment" is "at its origin an enjoinment to *repetition*."[43] For Santner, the "flood of talk" generating any symbolic identity depends on what he calls "ibidity"—the "citation" of the authority investing subjects with social recognition and "dignity, understood as the 'substance' generated by symbolic investiture." But because, Santner continues, "that authority is itself in some sense 'magical,' that is, unsubstantiated, without ultimate foundation in a final ground qua substantive reason, this 'ibidity' is, in the final analysis, a citation of lack, and so never settled once and for all."[44]

If symbolic identities are never "settled once and for all," then the southern citation of lack is, as I've argued, better understood as a citation of loss. There was no "getting over" the lost cause, no working through the death of Lee. Every replication of his image generated new melancholic attachments, such as lithographs printed to raise funds for a statue and shrine that, in turn, led to calls for a new and grander memorial that was eventually realized on Richmond's Monument Avenue. But Lee could be cited on behalf of different projects. For Early, embracing "the progressive spirit of the age" meant running "the ploughshare over the graves of our fathers." Would the southern people, he asks, turn their "backs upon the dead past," leave behind "dead issues and principles," as if "true principles ever die," and give up their "cherished traditions," their "civilization, and adopt the progressive civilization of the age"?[45] Early hoped not, but over time, veneration of the Confederate dead became more or less compatible with "progressive civilization." As early as 1866, Lee lent his name to a steamboat built in New Albany, Indiana. In 1921, Winston-Salem saw the grand opening of the Robert E. Lee Hotel. With the rise of the automobile, a Robert E. Lee motel located on Lee Highway in Bristol, Virginia, would house a restaurant operated by Harland Sanders in his precolonel phase. Today, thousands of Robert E. Lee T-shirts are available on the internet at a variety of price points.

The Memes of a Reconstructed People

According to Fellman (and as Douglass surely recognized), the apotheosis of an apolitical Lee not only justified white southerners in "their rule" but also provided "the whole nation with the sacrificial hero who was taken to define the deepest moral legacy of [the Civil War], with racial justice shunted aside by national white consensus."[46] Contemplation of Lee, then, meant looking away to an innocent Dixieland and looking away from the Southeast of the Reconstruction period. There, subjection to "negro government" or "negro rule"—the memes typically used to stigmatize Black participation in democratic government—bound in collective effort planter and poor white, firebreather and Unionist. White Republicans were not unknown, including General James Longstreet, whom Lee called his "old war horse." But his 1874 defense of the Republican-dominated Louisiana State House against White League assault made him a scalawag, and today his name is probably less familiar than that of Lee's actual horse.

Reconstruction was usually understood by southerners as a form of revenge. Albion Tourgée's novel *A Fool's Errand*, which drew on Tourgée's experiences as a legislator and judge in North Carolina, documents the humiliation of a people subjected to "enforced submission to the power of a people they had always deemed their inferiors,—the traditional foe of the South, the 'groveling and greedy Yankee,'—and then still further degraded by being placed on a level, in legal and political power and privilege, with a race despised beyond the power of language to express."[47] In a passage notable for its complete alignment with the southern perspective, Cash writes, "Not Ireland nor Poland, not Finland nor Bohemia, not one of the countries which prove the truth that there is no more sure way to make a nation than the brutal oppression of an honorably defeated people, not one of these, for all the massacres, the pillage, and the rapes to which they have so often been subjected, was ever so pointedly taken in the very core of its being as was the South."[48] Even more histrionically, Dixon calls Reconstruction a "second war" waged against "the unarmed people of the South, butchering the starving, the wounded, the women and children." This "attempt to establish with the bayonet an African barbarism on the ruins of Southern society was," he insists, "a conspiracy against human progress."[49]

Northerners generally found that of all Souths, this was the solidest. Of the Klan, Tourgée's narrator in *A Fool's Errand* notes that it represented the "whole South . . . fused and welded into one homogeneous mass, having one common thought, one imperial purpose, one relentless will."[50] Dixon agrees, attributing to the Klan the salvation of civilization itself.[51] But he says so only in the next century, while southerners of the time rarely did, disavowing the Klan as representative of the southern people, if not denying its existence altogether. Such dissembling had a practical purpose, since this construction of the "whole South" construed Klan activity (and racial terrorism more generally) as, in Tourgée's words, a "second rebellion." Like the first, this would presumably need to be put down by force. The risk was real, as evidenced by the passage of the Force Acts of 1870 and 1871, which effectively ended the Klan until its resurrection in 1915 following *Birth of a Nation*, itself a copy of Dixon's second novel of Reconstruction, *The Clansman* (1905).

Two other factors explain why the memes of white supremacy rarely coalesced into a notional South embraced by southerners. First, white supremacy was usually cited as an unremarkable and normative state of affairs conspicuous in the South only for its absence. In *The Lost Cause Regained*, Pollard insists that "white was the winning word, and let us never be done repeating it," but he intended the repetition to reassemble a "homogeneous" nation.[52] Similarly, the birth of Dixon's nation involved the United States of America, not a reconstituted Confederacy. More surprising, perhaps, were the similar conclusions reached by the abolitionist James Shepherd Pike, who predicted in *The Prostrate State* (1874) that South Carolina would become "Africanized" unless it "remain[ed] an integral part" of a federal union "incontestably white at the centre."[53] Writing of Reconstruction in *The Great South* (1875), Edward King sounds a similar note, declaring that "never before were a people, crushed to earth, kept down and throttled so long." "Tyrannical ignorance and carpet-baggery," according to King, had produced "revulsion" in the people of the South and ought to do the same in their northern counterparts: "The manliness which we received as a precious legacy with our Anglo-Saxon blood demands that we should cry out, 'Hold off your hands! Fair play!'"[54] Southerners generally agreed—indeed, insisted—that their blood was Anglo-Saxon, not (as it had often been before the war) Norman or Greco-Roman.

In other ways, the memes of white supremacy worked to reassemble a nation. Prior to the war, the slave power had threatened to transform the northern laborer into a slave. For Marcus M. "Brick" Pomeroy of Wisconsin, abolition threatened the same. An 1866 "soliloquy" from "A Poor Mechanic" shows the economic devastation caused by the war, while "A Freed Negro" rejoices that "dem fellars up Norf" would foot the bill for their lives of leisure: "Dey can pay taxes and support us. We's bin slaves long 'nough, now de white trash am slaves." Pomeroy's soliloquys were published as the sixth in a series of "Anti-Abolitionist Tracts," the second of which, "Free Negroism," purports to demonstrate that emancipation had been a "wretched and miserable failure, and that Negro Freedom is simply a tax upon White Labor."[55] Although this stigmatized version of "Negro Freedom" appealed mainly to working-class Democrats in the North, the idea that "negro rule" and "negro government" posed a threat attained, as Pike's and King's arguments suggest, broader acceptance among cultural elites. Although minimally reliable in describing Reconstruction governance—as C. Vann Woodward observes, "in no state did [the freedmen] hold place and power in anything approaching their actual numbers and voting strength"—these memes were powerful in forming alliances across sectional boundaries.[56] By the time William Dunning published his landmark historical study in 1907, an understanding of Reconstruction as a "struggle through which the southern whites, subjugated by adversaries of their own race, thwarted the scheme which threatened permanent subjection to another race" had, for many, come to seem self-evident.[57]

As the agent of interracial subjugation, the "carpetbagger" spread virally in the early years of Reconstruction. In 1868, Charles Chauncey Burr, the Copperhead editor of

New York's *Old Guard*, hoped the "southern people" would become "so mad" that they would "break the head of every 'carpet-bagger' who does not leave for his own regions."[58] William Lloyd Garrison, in equally measured tones, inveighs against the southern "reign of terror" waged on the "so-called 'carpet-baggers' of the North, who may hope for no mercy at the hands of the victorious rebels, who are never so jubilant as when burning negroes alive by a slow fire, or barbarously lynching Northern advocates of equal rights."[59] Eventually, however, the carpetbagger was "so-called" enough to crowd out competing notions of the men it named. Tourgée's narrator in *A Fool's Errand* complains that the term "instantly . . . spread through the press of the South" and that "with its usual subserviency . . . the North followed in its lead, and re-echoed its maledictions."[60] In an early literary appearance of the figure, John William De Forest introduces "Carpet-bagger Hunt," a "late convert" from New York machine politics who ventures south to make use of the freedman "as the monkey made use of the cat." De Forest, who had smiled at southern chivalry and provincialism, was not alone in his revulsion at the "carpet-bagger's guiding fingers" leading the freedman by his "uncertain nose."[61]

On the one hand, then, the memes of white supremacy supported the reassembly of a nation, as did reconciliationalist renderings of the war itself. In multiple venues, as David Blight has shown, the war was systematically "drained of evil, and to a great extent, of cause or political meaning."[62] In the literary domain, as Nina Silber argues, the courtship plot had evolved to produce endless variations of the "romance of reunion" wherein "symbolic marital alliance . . . became the principal representation of sectional reunion."[63] As Joyce Appleby has shown, "Northern novelists were the first to wave the olive branch" in their depiction of the war and its aftermath. Far from *following* the conciliatory rhetoric of southern writers, she argues that northern authors "actually originated it, introducing all the stilted clichés of intersectional romances, converted partisanships, and mutual respect for an opponent's heroism."[64] De Forest, for example, who had celebrated Lily Ravenel's conversion from secession to loyalty, published a later novel, *The Bloody Chasm* (1881), whose southern heroine is won over by a Union veteran. At a crucial moment in the courtship, he pens a poem celebrating the valor of the Confederate dead at Pickett's Charge:

> Five thousand were his heroes,
>   Three thousand those who bled;
> They marched without a shiver
> To join the knightly dead;[65]

While many romances avoided politics, a number aligned sectional reunion and conversion to the southern view of the "race problem." In his *The Shadow of the War* (1884), for example, Stephen T. Robinson, a physician from Edwardsville, Illinois, who had resided in South Carolina during Reconstruction, grafts a conventional romance plot onto what had emerged as the prevailing view of Reconstruction. Robinson's narrator is sharply critical of "Kukluxism," arguing that it "arose to degrade [the South's] civilization before the world" and also noting the economic ruin caused by the "arrogance" and "opulence" of the antebellum "oligarchy." Basil Gildersleeve, the Puritan protagonist of the novel, goes south believing that carpetbaggers are "martyrs" who "risked their lives in the cause of liberty" but comes to experience firsthand the horror of "carpet-bag rule." He pens a letter to the *Stalwart Republican* that goes unpublished:

> Day after day he closely watched the columns of the paper; but the letter never appeared. Instead, horrible stories of crime and race collisions, in which the white man was always the evil-doer, filled its pages. He saw numerous letters denunciatory of the South's unrelenting hatred for the North, and telling of the rough treatment both blacks and Northern men received at the hands of Southerners. He had once believed this trash to be the truth; but as he read it now in his new experience, he felt, not without some soul-sickness, that he had learned another lesson in worldly wisdom.

Eventually, he counsels his daughter, who is engaged to a local man, to withhold evidence of a lynching, since conviction of the guilty party would "consolidat[e] still more strongly the black vote on the side of this diabolical government."[66] The government in question belonged to South Carolina, which also provides the setting of De Forest's "The Colored Member" and the basis of King's commentary in *The Great South* and Pike's in *The Prostrate State*. If its experience of Reconstruction was anomalous—it housed, as Woodward documents, one of the very few legislative bodies comprising a majority of elected Black officials—South Carolina had, through sheer repetition, become the South's representative state.[67]

But even as more genteel notions of white supremacy facilitated sectional reconciliation, racial violence continued, as Tourgée's narrator suggests, to figure the war as an unfinished project and the South as a national aberration. Thomas Nast might use grotesque racist caricature to illustrate the disorder of "colored rule in a reconstructed state"—the state in question, again, being South Carolina—as he did in 1874.[68] But he could also pen in that same year a cartoon showing an African American family cowering as, above them, armed figures representing the White League and the Klan shake hands. According to the caption, "the Lost Cause" is "worse than the slavery," the "union as it was" having been shattered by the idea that "this is a white man's government."[69]

Southern *outrages*, often *rebel outrages*, continued to stigmatize the South, the lash of slavery mutating into new forms of racial violence that retained the moral taint of the peculiar institution. Although fictional, the reports of outrages in the *Stalwart Republican* reflect thousands of nonfictional variants in the Republican press. Typical is the Philadelphia *Evening Telegraph*'s denunciation of "outrages" committed by "the Rebels of the South," which it attributes, "at the bottom," to "the devilish spirit of caste—the notion that one man, because he is white, has a right to domineer

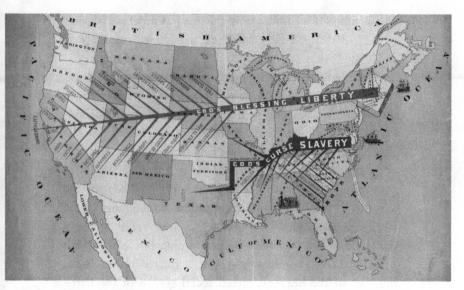

John F. Smith, *Historical Geography*, lithograph (Chicago: Orcutt Lithography, 1888). Courtesy of the Library of Congress.

over another because he is black."⁷⁰ The *Staunton (Va.) Vindicator* complains in 1869 that "Radical papers" inevitably styled "the acts of white men in the South [as] 'Rebel outrages,'" suggesting that "Radical Outrages" be used to mark the "horrible crimes perpetuated in different parts of the Southern country, upon white women, by depraved and wicked blacks."⁷¹ But despite such attempts to defeat the image of a savage and barbaric South by minimizing "so-called" outrages, outrages continued to mark it as such.

The stigmata marking a savage and barbaric South are neatly illustrated in an 1888 map that shows a tree representing slavery, "God's Curse," rooted at Jamestown, its crooked branches (avarice, lust, ignorance, sedition, and so forth) extending to "war" and, ultimately, "Hades." An overseer, lash in hand, appears in southern Alabama, leaving little doubt that racial violence continued to define the South's "historical geography." Rooted at Plymouth, the tree representing liberty, "God's Blessing," grows straight to "Immortality" (just west of California), bearing on its way the fruits of intelligence, virtue, morality, benevolence, and equal rights. If we understand this map as a pervasive form of interpellation we can understand, in part, why southerners rarely used white supremacy to define the group boundary.

The South's defensive posture relative to racial "outrages" is evident in a meme-rich series titled "Letters from the South," purportedly written by a "Northern Hypochondriac" and published in the *Southern Magazine* (1871). The series begins with a self-identified "ranting Abolitioner" and "freedom-shrieker"—a man "taught to *hate* the slave-compelling Southerner"—venturing south to "bear[d] the 'chivalry'" and "contem[n] the wrathful threatenings of the terrible 'Ku-Klux-Klan.'" Once there, however, he comes to understand that Wendell Phillips, trading birthplaces with Jefferson Davis, would surely have "expiated on the beauties . . . of the heaven-directed social system of the Patriarchs, as illustrated in relation of the inferior race of Ham to his natural Anglo-Saxon guide and master." For the narrator, a six-month sojourn effects a geographical cure. "Travel does take the nonsense out of one," he reports. What he had considered the *"curse"* of slavery stood revealed as "transmutation" of "the savages of Africa" from "the condition of ferocious beasts to civilized, utilised, Christianized 'Uncle Toms!'" Having answered the lingering accusations surrounding an institution no longer at issue, the northerner also finds that "hurry and skurry and eager haste," so prominent in the North, are nowhere to be found in the "sunny South."[72] But it bears noting that in putting a best (leisurely) foot forward, to borrow Tate's formulation, southerners continued to rest it on the neck of the formerly enslaved.

Melancholy and Markets

In "Letters from the South," mention of a "slower pace of life" (as we would now call it) is a way of indirectly answering the moral accusation still attached to slavery's curse. But it could also answer the curse's economic indictment: it might explain, in other words, why there was so little hurry and scurry in a New South quite as fantastic as the Old South it would invent. As the construction of Souths old and new proceeded, the soft memes of a slaveholding people survived unevenly. Some declined in importance, while others continued to mark a group different from the North. Dislodged from arguments over slavery and detached from the historical plantation, many acquired an abstract and more attenuated character. Often associated with a vanished past, some flourished within an emergent modern economy.

Some idea of the evolving South can be gathered from a fairly typical—indeed, altogether unremarkable—description of the southerner offered by S. H. Canfield in 1897. Writing in the *Washington (Ark.) Telegraph*, Canfield observes that "the Southerner was, and is, a man above the middle height," and a "gentleman" to boot. He "belonged to the old regime, . . . the antebellum regime, the slaveholding regime," but his "type exists in the South today." Having "not a drop of foreign blood in his veins," he "looks like a transplanted Englishman . . . modified by some centuries of climate." He "carries himself unobtrusively and leaves the swagger to the negro out for a Sunday holiday." Like "the New Englander, who is his antithesis in many ways," he speaks "the best English," but sounds different. He "comes of agricultural stock" and is "devoted to the chase." "By birth and breeding chivalric," he will "remain so"—at least Canfield "hope[s] that he will." This is why, Mark Twain's belief notwithstanding, the "popularity of Scott was an effect, not a cause." The southerner takes a "less commercial view of life," and transacts business "in great degree by word of mouth." At least this is true in the "country communities," there being "no marked difference between the business method of Atlanta and Boston." He places "the female of the species on a pedestal" and stands ready to protect the homestead, employing, if necessary, the "silent sentinel of the fireside—the shotgun."[73]

Between the current type and his predecessor in the old regime, there is obvious continuity but difference as well.

Presented as a copy, the present-day southerner seems almost a shadow of the original. Removed from both the old plantation and modern centers of commerce (including Atlanta), he, unlike his predecessor, seems unlikely to dominate the nation. Adjacent articles in the *Telegraph* suggest his disadvantage. One proclaims, rather too enthusiastically, that the state of Arkansas has "more of the elements of empire[,] more variegated resources than perhaps any other state in the Union"; another brags that the southern railway had acquired "the three biggest and strongest passenger locomotives in the whole world."[74] In suggesting, on the one hand, that the old regime had, in the form of the southerner, survived intact, and, on the two others, that the South stood poised to flourish in a new and modern world, the *Telegraph* sends different messages, neither persuasive.

Within this domain marked by loss and aspiration, memes mutated, giving rise to new representations of the character of the South. Hospitality became less associated with practices of housing guests and more associated with, as a recent Pinterest meme has it, "not a tangible thing, but an attitude which has been ingrained in southerners forever . . . a way of life that lets people be as warm as the climate."[75] For Governor John B. Gordon of Georgia, speaking at an 1887 Memorial Day meeting of the Confederate Survivors' Association, "gone forever" was "that old plantation life—gone with its perennial hospitality" once "as free and boundless as the vitalizing air around us." "Gone, too" was "our peculiar and characteristic civilization," one that had, nonetheless, "left its ineffaceable impression on the character of the people."[76] In another speech at the same event, Charles C. Jones enjoins his audience to "render tribute to the virtues of our Confederate dead" and to honor the "holy memories which are here enshrined." But he further exhorts his "beloved South" to remain a "peculiar people—peculiar in its conceptions and manifestations" of "hospitality, of honor toward God and man, of devotion to exalted womanhood."[77] Melancholic attachment to a lost southern hospitality, itself attached to the lost cause, helped to ensure its replication. In 1874, the Confederate diplomat Edwin De Leon insists that southern hospitality "but 'languishingly live[s],'" as the "unbounded hospitality, and the organised labor system, which assimilated the 'landed gentry' of our Southern country so closely to their old English prototypes, are fast disappearing, and the next generation will know them by hearsay only." For De Leon, it was evident that "the old plantation life, as it existed before the war for two generations, is vanishing as rapidly into the twilight region of romance and recollection."[78] To the contrary, the "old plantation life" did not vanish into but reproduced virally within that twilight region, and in ways fully consonant with an emergent industrial economy. For Jones, the southern people would remain peculiar only if the "South remain purged of all modern commercial methods" and resistant to "the consummation of soulless, gainful consolidations."[79] But this was mere talk, and soon hospitality would be incorporated into what Grace Elizabeth Hale calls "DixieBrand, a regional identity made or marketed as southern" that regularly incorporated romanticized images of Black labor, plantation homes, and Confederate iconography.[80] As with Lee, southern hospitality would eventually find its way to the hotel. That, in 1995, 91.5% of southerners and 89.5% of non-southerners rated southern hospitality as somewhat or very important to their "definition of today's South" is surely attributable, and in large measure, to the number of market transactions involving the idea and its association with the "old plantation life."[81] Time would prove the spectral value of a world gone with the wind.

Mollie, a character in Tourgée's 1880 novel *Bricks without Straw* remarks that "in that mystically-bounded region known as 'the South,'" the "people were first of all 'Southerners'" and last of all Americans. This was clear because "the word 'Southern' leaps into prominence as soon as the old 'Mason and Dixon's line is crossed." There, she observes, "'southern was invariably attached to railroads, steamboats, stage-coaches, express companies, books, news-papers, patent-medicines, churches, manners, gentlemen, la-dies, restaurants, bar-rooms, whisky, gambling-hells, and principles." "Everything," Mollie concludes, that "courts popularity, patronage, or applause, makes haste to brand it-self as distinctively and specifically 'Southern.'"[82]

That the memes of Dixie attached easily to commodities suggests a function more identitarian than ideological. For De Leon and Gordon, as for the proslavery theorists, south-ern hospitality depended on a particular "organized labor system," which (also like those theorists) De Leon imag-ines as hewing to an "old English prototype."[83] The erro-neous assumption that southern traits require a particular economic base has persisted in the conservative tradition of southern thought. For the Nashville Agrarians, agrarian values depended upon an agrarian economy, while Eugene Genovese scoffs at "philosophical idealists" who "seem to think that [agrarian] values could be defended or restored despite the triumph of bourgeois social relations and an at-tendant, self-revolutionizing economic system that has his-torically proven itself a solvent of those very values."[84] And yet "those very values"—generally vague ones—have dura-bly constituted groups opposing "modernity," whatever its particular materialist incarnation at a given historical mo-ment. Always the value (or cultural trait) "languishingly lives," detached from its purported economic base; always its demise is announced; always it continues to define the group boundary. In this way, Dixie memes have reliably as-sembled groups of southerners through different regimes of labor ranging from chattel slavery to the flexible labor of the contemporary hospitality industry.

Particular memes were often explicitly embedded in dis-courses of modernity. Self-evidently anachronistic, "chiv-alry" provided the *Nation* opportunity to sneer at the South. A ring tournament in 1866 revealed men who "dressed up in fantastic costumes" and who "call[ed] themselves 'disin-herited knights,' 'knights of the sword,' 'knights of the lone star,' and pretend[ed] to worship a young woman from a modest wooden house in the neighborhood as the 'queen of love and beauty.'" "We need not," it continues, "have the least hesitation in pronouncing [southern society] semi-civilized, as still in a stage much behind what a distinguished French writer calls a 'vrai people moderne.'"[85] Although conservatives such as Albert Taylor Bledsoe might answer the charge heatedly, progressives like Pollard (in his post–lost cause phase) were more ambivalent, noting that "southern chivalry" often described what was merely "a low physical courage." Other "noble virtues" evident in "the people of the South" but that "the commercial spirit of the age has elsewhere outgrown," carried, according to Pollard, "the peculiar faults of an *untravelled* people—a people who pass their lives in local neighborhoods, and who hav[e] but little idea of how large and various the world is." "The worst faults of the Southern mind," he concludes, "are to be traced to the isolation of agricultural pursuits and to peculiar habits of local attachment added to that."[86]

Although chivalry remained a defining characteristic of the members of the Confederate pantheon, accusations of provincialism and backwardness may have led to its decline as a group marker. As early as 1871, the Memphis *Public Ledger* adduces the rise of "barbeques and picnics raging throughout the Southern States" as evidence that the "age of chivalry, wherein young men tilted at rings and called it a tournament, has passed away."[87] Another factor, as Daniel R. Weinfeld has suggested, may have been the rise of Black jousting tournaments in the years after the war. Of one such event, Weinfeld reports, a southern magazine wrote "young [white] men who had ridden in previous tournaments felt indignant that their recent servants should usurp their noble pastime"; of another, a Memphis newspaper suggested that "Northern people" were encouraging a "little fun" at the expense of white southern "chivalry."[88] Whatever the cause, the print frequency of the phrase "southern chivalry" peaked in the late 1860s, and ring tournaments declined in popularity, their latest iterations in the 1880s advertised playfully in a spirit of creative anachronism.

Although contested by progressives such Pollard, Grady, and Dixon, localism, by contrast, mutated and remained a durable marker of the southern group. As Lloyd Pratt observes, "This notion that locality governs southern culture has dominated the history of the U.S. South. Whether it gets figured as the nation's region, or our South, or the real South, this thing called southern locality just will not go away."[89] But persistence should not be confused with either distinctiveness or similarity over time. As Arjun Appadurai suggests, the story of locality recently "under siege" is an old and universal tale, and its inward focus conceals, invariably, that the production of locality "contains or implies a theory of context; a theory, in other words, of what a neighborhood is produced from, against, in spite of, and in relation to."[90] To be a southern locality, as opposed to a merely local one, requires that a variant of the North be on the other side of it. The pattern is evident as early as Augustus Baldwin Longstreet's *Georgia Scenes* (1835), which presents the town of Springfield as "admitting frankly, that living as she had always lived, right amidst gullies, vapours, fogs, creeks, and lagoons, she was wholly incapable of comprehending that expansive kind of benevolence, which taught her to love people whom she knew nothing about, as much as her next door neighbors and friends." Springfield's rival, Campbellton, takes a different approach, believing that under the Federal Constitution, "the several towns of the confederacy should . . . la[y] down all former prejudices and jealousies, as a sacrifice on the altar of their country . . . be united in a single body." That the dispute isn't local at all becomes clear when Campbellton is "literally *nullified*," a clear nod to the nullification crisis of the 1830s.[91] At its height, Longstreet observes that he "saw the champions of the South defeated again and again. I saw them driven by the noise of a letter from positions, which would have been impregnable to a nobler enemy. I witnessed such defeats until the Union lost its beauty in my eyes, and Civil War lost its deformity."[92] Loving one's neighbors more than strangers is thus enlisted on behalf of the southern "position." This claim is, one the one hand, conceptually incoherent, given that there are plenty of strangers in the South and in Georgia, the particular state Longstreet sought to defend in the *State Rights Sentinel*, where the sketch originally appeared. But it's also, on the other, rhetorically powerful in its proposition that if you don't support nullification and states' rights, you clearly don't love your neighbors.[93]

In this crude attempt to bind localism to sectionalism, community to imagined community, we find the basic template for the evolution of localist memes in the prewar era. To be sure, nullification provided only a temporary and uneven basis for the assembly of southerners. Longstreet quarreled not just with the North, but with Virginia and the governor of his own state. Nullification remained a matter of disagreement, not difference, and there evolved no conception of a nullifying people made so by nature. Slavery, by contrast, more reliably explained how the locality was southern. As George Washington Cable observes in 1882, the region "was turned by the plantation idea into a vast archipelago of patriarchal states whereof every one was a complete empire within itself."[94] In John Pendleton Kennedy's *Swallow Barn*, the planter Frank Meriwether proclaims that bad roads make good Virginians. For the planter, roads and steamships lead, ominously, to "the annihilation of space"—a thing decidedly "not to be desired."[95] Michael O'Brien observes in Calhoun the "tendency . . . of seeing the world of slavery as a series of island communities, as small worlds presided over by a patriarchal master, around whose feet clustered wife and children, overseer and slaves." This was helpful to the defense of slavery, "for if," O'Brien argues, "the essence of modernity was interconnection, making slavery patriarchal and so socially isolated made it plausibly antimodern."[96]

It is crucial, however, to recognize that the plausible antimodernity of a slaveholding people was neither static nor complacent. As proslavery apologists frequently insisted, replication of the plantation unit had driven westward expansion. Localism could itself be mobile, since an island in the plantation archipelago might be swapped out for another with richer soil. Nor did traditionalism carry any taint of provincialism or economic backwardness. The slave order was sturdy and muscular, a time-tested system free of capitalist modernity's peculiar fragilities—its pathological isms, labor anxieties, and social unrest.[97] Since cotton was king, the plantation archipelago produced kinglike men and, through them, a superior people—superior *because*, as John Henry Hammond insists in his mudsill speech, "we are old-fashioned at the South yet."[98] This notion of a rugged and durable provincialism survived the war for a brief time, as can be seen in Bledsoe's suggestion that the South, being a "rural population," was more isolated and individualistic than the North and that these traits were "the nursery of all virtue, and of all greatness of men." By "universal consent," he insisted, "an agricultural population has always been deemed the most virtuous, and their characteristics, whatever they may be, the most unchangeable."[99]

But Hammond's agrarian South, unlike Bledsoe's, was to be defended by arms. This locality was the hearthstone defended by the Confederate soldier, the unabstracted community for which, according to Tate, Lee fought. A version of this locality would reappear during Reconstruction, when the South was invaded by carpetbaggers and later during the civil rights era, when the threat would come from the outside agitator. But locality also evolved into an abstraction to be cherished, not just defended. As Bledsoe demonstrates, rural isolation could be causally linked to the unchangeable character of an agricultural people, and without inviting reprisal. But with cotton dethroned, agrarianism and localism were harder to associate with southern greatness. The promise of the New South having been unrealized, the South was old fashioned because it had to be and because being so answered allegations of provincialism and backwardness. If lack could be construed as what the Yankees had stolen, it could also be recuperated as virtue, as impervious to Yankee theft. As Noel Polk argues, "rootedness, a fixation to a geographical 'place,' and a devotion to the rural" evolved as virtues made of necessity, deriving, in all likelihood, from "southerners' financial limitations."[100] Even so, southerners perpetuated, as Ted Ownby observes, "the pre-Civil War tradition of writing as if poverty did not exist," the idea of a "South without poverty" culminating in *I'll Take My Stand*, which proffered farms bursting with agrarian abundance.[101] For Allen Tate, growing up in a "pre-industrial society" that was "backward and Southern" meant that one's "identity had everything to do with land and material property, at a definite place, and very little to do with money."[102] On a professor's salary, however, he moved frequently, never to a farm but once, briefly, to a house in my neighborhood most recently marketed by Allen Tate Realty (no relation). As O'Brien observes, for all the talk of a home place, "Southern realtors are not noticeable impoverished."[103]

Memes made of necessity often acquired a sacred, mystical character. Southern *place* mutated into something purportedly timeless at the same time as the world, according to Max Weber, became disenchanted—literally, "demagicalized"—owing to the rise of commercialism and bureaucratic management. In its enchanted form, place was often attached to what Edward King characterizes as "picturesque and unjust civilization of the past," and rarely to its opposite, "the prosaic and leveling civilization of the present."[104] To the narrator of Thomas Nelson Page's "Marse Chan," the "character of the race" whose plantation ruins he contemplated was best explained by their "proud seclusion," their stillness as "the outer world strode by them while they dreamed." The magic of that vanished way of life could, as ruin, become the imagined property of all southerners, not just those whose grandfathers had owned these "splendid mansions."[105] Lost in its immediately reality, the plantation of the Old South retained, in Žižek's terms, its "notional essence" as melancholic anchor.[106]

At a more abstract and generic level, melancholic longing for *place* reflected efforts by peoples across the world to imagine their special and threatened qualities as they adapted to industrialized economies. As Svetlana Boym shows in *The Future of Nostalgia*, "longing for home became a central trope of romantic nationalism," with different nations claiming that "they had a special word for homesickness that was radically untranslatable."[107] Although the South never coined a special word, Thomas Wolfe's *You Can't Go Home Again* has often assured southerners of their exceptional exile. Alternatively, access *to* home can serve as a distinguishing characteristic, as it does for David Mathews: "Southerners have a unique sense of time and place, of belonging, of community. Southerners have roots. They have an identity. A Southerner—whatever his station, whatever his color—has a 'home.'"[108] Or place can be posed as spectral. In similarly overwrought prose, John William Corrigan and Miller Williams write that "the landscape of the South that is most haunted is within the Southern man. And there, too, the ghosts have names. The have been named before, and the names are not ours, but they are good and honest names. They are Religion and History, Place and Responsibility."[109]

The crucial feature of such claims is not that they are true but that they are unfalsifiable, "home" and "place" having as little relation to actual buildings or locations as "soil" or "the land" have to dirt. Mathews isn't saying that no southerner is unhoused but offering a kind of prayer invoking sacralized senses southerners are said to uniquely possess. For Corrigan and Williams, it's a matter of haunting, not possession, but the particulars of such liturgies are incidental. What's important is that they "have been named before" and compel repetition. To the outsider, such statements are likely to appear absurd, but for the insider—the believer—citation appears as inheritance, affectively binding the subject to the group imaginary by purporting to delineate its boundary. In this way, the free-floating nature of abstractions such as place can facilitate their replication as articles of faith, invoking a "ground of commonality" that, to belabor a point, doesn't come from the ground up.

Reconstructing the Plantation

The shift toward abstraction, however, did not render localist and traditionalist memes inconsequential. Prayers can also be flags, and what southerners rallied around was, indirectly, an emergent regime of Black disfranchisement and segregation that within the space of a few decades was rendered "timeless and inevitable" by place and its adjuncts. This functionality is apparent in Charles Reagan Wilson's "Place, Sense of" entry in *The Encyclopedia of Southern Culture*, which begins by noting that "the term *sense of place* as used in the South implies an organic society. Until recently southern whites frequently used *place* to indicate the status of blacks."[110] The transition would be startling were it not for the fact that the society's most distinctive and organic feature was its racial hierarchy. As Robert Brinkmeyer observes, "to celebrate place suggests celebrating stasis and the status quo, perhaps one reason that segregation, with its barriers controlling not only movement in space but also within the social and economic spheres, seemed so natural in the South."[111]

Noting a similar moment in Wilson's entry on manners, Werner Sollors reports that "one finds the description of the South as 'polite, courteous, kind, gentle, hospitable, friendly yet dignified,' alongside the information that 'etiquette required whites to behave in certain ways toward blacks, ways seemingly at odds with their normal code of *good* manners.'"[112] "A breech of racial manners by a black man," Wilson writes, "could lead to a tongue-lashing, humiliation, and sometimes violence."[113] In both instances, the "good" version of the meme seems to require acknowledgment of its underside, as if, in Roland Barthes's words, the "contents of the collective imagination" might be protected "by means of a small inoculation of acknowledged evil."[114] But in the age of Jim Crow, the conceptualization of place and manners as group markers required the erasure of their disciplinary function within the habitus. If the everyday world of the Southeast, *place* indicated where Black persons should remain and *manners* were a way of keeping them there, in the *South*, their notional essence confirmed the settled and organic nature of the social order.

In time, "community" would name the local instance of this South held in common, each person in their proper place. It was usually realized in a small town, which replaced the plantation as the "the molecular unit, the very quintessence, of the South and of southernism." Until a few decades ago, community could be located in almost any southern novel, even one with a lynching.[115] For Cleanth Brooks, "a true community (a *gemeinschaft*) is held together by manners and morals deriving from a commonly held view of reality."[116] On the ground, it was less clear that everyone saw things the same way, and everyday encounters could be fraught. But from a height and with the right distortion, the collective vision could appear sharper, the enchantment more compelling. Once in proper view, place, manners, and community might also be wielded against the North, where atomized humanity wandered the bleak terrain of the modern *gesellschaft*, encountering alienation and indifference at every turn.

Racial disorder proved the primary obstacle to this vision. In 1908, the Harvard philosopher Josiah Royce describes having "long learned from my Southern friends" that interracial comity could "only be attained by a firm and by a very constant and explicit insistence upon keeping the negro in his proper place, as a social inferior—who, then, as an inferior, should, of course, be treated humanely, but who must first be clearly and unmistakably taught where he belongs."[117] From his southern friends, however, he might also have learned that such instruction was unnecessary, the social hierarchy having evolved as a natural and consensual order. The old cornerstone of slavery having been shattered, a new one had emerged to ground, through the regime of segregation, Alexander Stephens's "great truth": "that the negro is not equal to the white man; that . . . subordination to the superior race—is his natural and normal condition."

As scholars from C. Vann Woodward to Adolph Reed have shown, the ascent of Jim Crow was both strange and short, and its success depended in part on developing, as feudalism had done for slavery, a backstory that was continuous with the present and that rendered it inevitable.[118] "Before the civil war," William Graham Sumner remarks in 1907, "whites and blacks had formed habits of action and feeling toward each. They lived in peace and concord, and each one grew up in the ways which were traditional and customary." Attempts to alter these habits through legislation were, he declares, in "vain." History had shown, William Archibald Dunning similarly insists, that the place of slavery "must be taken by some set of conditions which, if more humane and beneficent in accidents, must in essence express the same fact of racial inequality" and thus make possible the "coexistence in one society of two races so distinct in character as to render coalescence impossible."[119] Thus for Sumner, a sociologist at Yale, Jim Crow was made up of *mores*, while for Dunning, a historian at Columbia, the "undoing of reconstruction" (itself an "undoing" of an organic relation) was a foregone conclusion.

These conclusions floated on a sea of citation, some of it modern and scientific in nature. When, for example, Grady declares there to be "an instinct, ineradicable and positive, that will keep the races apart," he isn't just responding to George Washington Cable's specific assertion that "race instinct" was "pure twaddle" or to more pervasive accusations of "race prejudice" (a term that, like "racism" today, carried a heavy stigma).[120] Speaking for "We of the South," Grady cites a scientific principle to disabuse his reader of any notion that "the soul of the South . . . breathes through Mr. Cable's repentant sentences."[121] In defending white supremacy as based in nature—as "bred in the bone and blood"—Grady had at his disposal a broadly accepted body of knowledge.[122] Unnecessary and largely avoided in the defense of slavery, scientific racism proved useful in support of racial apartheid. Hinton Rowan Helper, who had inveighed against the slave power and the "lords of the lash," sought, like Pollard, to reconfigure a conflict between South and North into one between white and black. Contemporary anthropology—Josiah Nott, Louis Agassiz, Samuel George Morton—offered him the "consolation" that the Black race "shall all speedily pass away . . . [to] be known only, if known at all, in fossil form!"[123] Race instinct formed part of this knowledge, which was by no means limited to the South. J. H. Van Evrie, a Canadian-born physician, claims in 1868 that "the American, with the instinct of race to guide him, with the natural sense of superiority over these Indians, negroes, or hybrids, was impelled by nature herself to assert his supremacy." Against this instinct, the "Northern states . . . are striving to 'reconstruct' American society on a Mongrel basis," thus dooming "the Southern people to a fate more horrible than death itself!"[124] Writing in the aftermath of Reconstruction and on the cusp of Jim Crow, Grady uses the idea to naturalize a voluntary and equitable separation of the races. Similarly, A. A. Gundy argues that segregated schools were prompted by "a divine race instinct and not prejudice." That prejudice was not the cause could be seen, Gundy suggests, by the fact that local white teachers happily taught "black children on the west coast of Africa" and "Indians in South America," even if "at home would have shirked from teaching negroes," again, "not from hatred or prejudice."[125]

But if science could be cited in support of the southern way of life, its organicism more often depended on the white magic of moonlight and magnolias. Representations of *what slavery had been* evolved rapidly and in close concert with the rise of Jim Crow. It was this world that Reconstruction had destroyed, a world in which the true "character and disposition [of the negro]" hadn't yet "been perverted and poisoned by designing schemers," as Gundy puts it.[126] The invention of the Old South by the New is a twice-told tale, but it is important to emphasize that the plantation memeplex still recognizable today is, as Lucinda MacKethan and others have argued, substantially the creation of the late nineteenth century.[127] Relatively few in number, the proto-"mammies" and "uncles" of antebellum plantation fiction differ substantially from their postwar counterparts. Certain conventions, to be sure, persist, notably the calibrated backtalk practiced by enslaved characters. In disputation with his master, *Swallow Barn*'s Carey, for example, "feels himself authorized to maintain his positions according to the freest parliamentary form, and sometimes with a violence of asseveration that compels his master to abandon his ground, purely out of faint-heartedness."[128] Similarly, Aunt Kizzy in Caroline Lee Hentz's *The Planter's Northern Bride* joins household conversations "with the freedom of a privileged member of the family."[129] Such familiarity answered the charge of the British abolitionist William Whewell that "slavery converts a person into a thing—a subject merely passive, without any of the recognized attributes of human nature."[130] But evidence of slavery's "moral relation" often came with caveats: Carey is a buffoon easily manipulated with small favors, while Aunt Kizzy is seduced by the religious enthusiasm of a disguised abolitionist, failing in one instance her "positive duty" to care for the family's infant.[131] Occasionally, the moral relation could be corrupted, as in Longstreet's "The 'Charming Creature' as Wife," where a husband is vexed by his servants' "idleness, their insolence, and their disgusting familiarities with his wife."[132] More typical, however, is the comical impudence of Francis James Robinson's Old Jack C—, which requires narrative explanation: "To the superficial observer, Jack has the appearance of being too impudent for a slave, but those who know him best, and who can thus better appreciate his eccentricities by this knowledge, know him to be an obedient and industrious servant; contented in his station in life, and with not the shadow of a wish to change it."[133] Offered such a chance, Tom in Simms's *Woodcraft* "cunningly reject[s]" freedom by declaring to his master Porgy that "ef *I* doesn't belong to *you*, *you* b'longs to *me*!" A "sly shake of the head" suggests that has less to do with the "lub" he proclaims for his master than the pragmatism of a good deal. Porgy will provide dinner; Tom will cook it; both will eat.[134]

Generally absent, however, is what would become crucial after slavery: the notion that slave labor was characterized not just by consent and reciprocity but by loyalty and selfless devotion.[135] The "expression of indescribable solicitude and love" with which an "ancient pair of eyes" views a former master in in James Lane Allen's 1888 story "Two Kentucky Gentlemen of the Old School" would have been familiar to American readers at this time. [136] Indeed, it was a motif of the issue of the *Century* in which Allen's story appeared. In a poem by Thomas Nelson Page also published in this issue a freedman, addressing his master's son, reminiscences about the days before "de war":

> When I was born, you' gran'pa gi' me to your Marse Phil,
> To be his body-servant like, you know;
> An' we growed up togerr, like two stalks in one hill,
> Bofe tasslin' an' den shootin' in de row.[137]

Of the mammy, Page observes in 1892 that she "received, as she gave, an unqualified affection; if she was a slave, she at least was not a servant, but was an honored member of the family, universally beloved, universally cared for."[138] In a similar vein, John Fox Jr. offers an elegy to "Aunt Dinah," a "pillar" of "the social system of the South." "But for Aunt Dinah," he asks, "would the master have had the heart for such hospitality? Would the guest have found it so hard to get away?" Banished to the past—"She is gone," Fox laments—the mammy invoked a lost and potentially recoverable ideal of devoted servility.[139] According to Cheryl Thurber, the mammy figure peaked in southern memoirs in the early decades of the twentieth century, a time when writers "tended to glorify the mammy in the abstract, as the idea rather than as a person."[140] In 1911, the *Savannah Tribune* published a poem declaring that "when the last black mammy's gone she'll never come again"—although, somewhere "beyond earth's woe and wile," her "dear ole arms will fold again o' Mistus and 'her chile.'" A "Black Mammy Memorial" planned in Athens, Georgia, detailed in an article that tellingly accompanies the poem, is proffered as "evidence of appreciation of the old, antebellum Negro." An adjacent institute would train Black students in housekeeping, cooking, sewing, and laundering, clearly marking the terms of what the newspaper labels a "racial peace monument."[141] Kentuckian William Lightfoot Visscher locates his "Black Mammy" in an antebellum world absent the curse of free labor. There,

> Contentment rules, with guileless glee,
> A synonym, for them, of "free,"
> Their liberty was greater then
> That that of many "hired men,"[142]

As with the lost cause, print iterations led to stone. A monument titled "To the Faithful Slaves of the Confederacy" was erected in Fort Mill, South Carolina, in 1896, to be followed in 1914 by a frieze on the Confederate Monument at Arlington National Cemetery showing a mammy receiving an infant from a departing Confederate soldier.

The mammy's propagandistic function was fully evident to Black Americans. When, in 1923, Senator John Williams of Mississippi proposed a monument on the National Mall "in memory of the faithful, colored mammies of the South," the legislation was voted down in the House of Representatives largely due to opposition from the NAACP and the National Association of Colored Women's Club. As M. M. Manring shows in his study of the nation's most widely replicated mammy, Aunt Jemima was viewed with hostility by Black Americans from her introduction at the 1893 World's Fair in Chicago.[143]

It would be a mistake, however, to view the mammy as a lie that bound. In the voice of an imagined southerner, W. J. Cash writes that "here about us in this very hour of new freedom and bitter strife are hundreds of worn-out Uncle Toms and black mammies still clinging stubbornly to the old masters who can no longer feed them, ten thousand Jim Crows, still kicking their heels and whooping for the smile of a black man. Hate him? My good friend, we love him dearly—and we alone, for we alone know him."[144] The reign of Uncle Remus depended largely, as Jeremy Wells argues, on Harris's ability to signal his deep understanding of Black culture while also suggesting that he couldn't "convey the full measure of what it has to say."[145] In his effort to explain the coexistence of the "race instinct" and interracial goodwill, Grady finds himself "tempted into trying to explain here what I never yet seen a stranger to the South able to understand."[146] The idea that "the relations of the Southern people with the negro are close and cordial," as Grady insists in his 1888 "New South" address, constituted a kind of race knowledge that outsiders, presumably, found hard to grasp. Cash correctly claims that southerners "believed in their professions" on this front and, moreover, "loved the thing."[147] As Barthes suggests, to view myth as either symbol or alibi is "to destroy the myth, either by making its intention obvious, or by unmasking . . . and demystifying" it.[148] Loving the mystification ensured its functionality. Whether grounded in a particular copy of the mammy or one more broadly connected to the bygone plantation, the fantasy of interracial comity effectively reconstructed the South, maintaining the group through a kind of anamorphosis—a distorted image that, when viewed from a certain point of view, appears in perfect proportion.

To be clear, the group so bound remained racially exclusive. Although the mammy or uncle might figure in an interracial "family," identitarian uses of "South" and "southern" excluded, with few exceptions, persons of color. Although Black persons might be of the South, in the South, or from the South, they were rarely southerners. Gundy dwells on the "beneficence of the southern people," finding himself unable "to place their friendship for the negro race second to any." He loved Cash's "thing," reflecting on the "self-sacrifice, the loss, the endurance, and the true nobility of soul involved in the efforts" to uplift "the negroes of the South." They, in turn, would reciprocate by "admir[ing] and trust[ing], and even ador[ing] their white neighbors as their truest and purest friends."[149] "The South is a single, homogenous people," *The Library of Southern Literature* affirms in 1907 in the preface to the first of sixteen volumes that, all-told, offer as evidence 574 authors, none of them Black.[150]

Black writers made similar assumptions. Anna Julia Cooper announces herself as a "voice from the South" but claims that "the Southern woman" would resist political alignment with "the Black woman." Although "the Southerner is not a cold-blooded victim," she complains that "Southern influence, Southern ideas, and Southern ideals" had "dictated to and domineered over" the nation, "the Southerner . . . shaping the policy of this government to suit his purpose." In a single exception, she jabs at the "reasoning powers" of the "Southern woman" and asks pardon, "being one myself."[151] The joke depends on her presumed exclusion from the category. In *The Souls of Black Folk*, W. E. B. Du Bois declares that "the South is not 'solid'" but assumes, similarly, that it is white. Black men should "judge the South discriminatingly" by recognizing that the "present generation of Southerners are not responsible for the past," and in particular for the postwar era, when "the South believed an educated Negro to be a dangerous Negro." Du Bois views the "recent course of the South toward Negroes" as "nauseating" yet insists that "the imperative duty of thinking black men" was not to "inveigh indiscriminately against 'the South'" but to adjust criticism to specific leaders: to, for example, argue with Thomas Nelson Page, denounce Ben Tillman, and praise Charles B. Aycock.[152] In *The Red Record*, Ida B. Wells-Barnett occasionally references an implicitly white "South" and "southerner," describing, for example, "the southerners' method of dealing with the Negro." She explains how southerners defend "their lawlessness" and catalogs "the unjust practices of the South against the Negro." More often, however, she uses "white" to modify those terms. She refers repeatedly to "the southern white man" and reports a horrific lynching in Carrolton, Alabama committed by "honorable white southerners" who "resent 'outside interference.'"[153] By contrast, there are no "black southerners" or "southern black men." Perhaps cagiest of all was, unsurprisingly, Booker T. Washington, who contrasts "the black man and the Southern white man" but usually takes pains to avoid an implicitly white South. Most often the South is merely a geographical expression, and, like Wells-Barnett, he typically refers to "Southern whites" and "Southern white people." But also like her, he avoids linking "Black" and "southern," coming closest to doing so in announcing his preference for a hypothetical "audience of Southern people, of either race, together or taken separately."[154] In Washington's strategic effort to enlist whites as allies, this made sense, but for most of his Black contemporaries, southerners constituted an antigroup, if not an outright enemy. As O'Brien argues, the South has ever "only made certain people Southerners," and it was not until the 1960s that significant numbers of Black persons living in the region were willing to describe themselves using the term "southern."[155]

But doesn't it follow from the argument that plantation memes are best understood within the process of (white) group formation—that is, as yet another flag to rally around, another object of veneration, another set of talking points to be wielded against the stigmata of the North—that they seep into the habitus as well? Just as for Tate and Genovese, the idea of feudalism produced a feudal society and for Cash the image of the planter came to be the planter, did the broad replication of mammy and uncle provide a kind of script, a set of expectations, shaping the domain of what goes without saying? The idealist position has been argued by a number of commentators, most notoriously Stanley Elkins, who views "Sambo" as blurring "the line between 'accommodation' (as conscious hypocrisy) and behavior inextricable from basic personality."[156] For Trudier Harris, the mammy type in Charles Chesnutt's *Marrow of Tradition* "reflect[s] the historical pattern of many black women after Reconstruction, women who found themselves without identities beyond those of the white families for whom they had spent most of their lives working."[157] Jefferson Humphries lends reality to fiction through seven "narrative characterizations" despite acknowledging that the South is "only related to geographical place by pure arbitrary contingency." After briefly outlining these—Thomas Jefferson, Edgar Poe/Roderick Usher, Sut Lovingood, Robert E. Lee, Uncle Remus and Aunt Jemima/Nat Turner, the belle, and the "southern middle class"—he asks, rhetorically, "if any reasonable person who knows any part of the South today . . . can deny that the types, the narrative characterizations I just listed, continue to determine and therefore describe accurately (or to describe accurately and therefore determine) much of the appearance, comportment, and ideology of persons living today from Virginia to Texas?"[158] Partly, I view the idealist argument skeptically because, by Jefferson's standard, I'm unreasonable. Of the people I know, very few conform to his typology; of those most are concentrated in the "Sut Lovingood" and "belle" groupings, and none is typologically "determined" by Uncle Remus or Aunt Jemima. Mostly, however, I suspect that these *kinds of persons* are less effective in creating persons *of these kinds* than in underwriting an idea of a group to whom they are important.

To be clear, I do not claim an altogether arbitrary relationship between meme and habitus. As noted, I know many people for whom the redneck type, at least in its performative dimensions, seems related to appearance, comportment, and even ideology. And it's possible that, had I been born in rural Georgia, where my grandparents lived, the shadow of Scarlett O'Hara would have fallen more heavily. But even conceding Humphries's argument that all southerners are merely players, there is no reason to assume a southern stage in the first place—that is, unless the "geographical place" has organically produced the types prior to becoming "related to geographical place by pure arbitrary contingency." In order to reintegrate a coherent South (*the place* where everyone is inevitably a *kind of person*) Humphries must erase the memes' historical specificity—the conditions under which they emerged, mutated, and functioned—and, at the same time, assume that they will replicate in perpetuity. But if the South is indeed a "lie, a fiction to which we've lent reality by believing it," it would seem important to consider the origin and function of its constitutive fictions and to ask whether our belief is lending reality to the right lies. With respect to Uncle Remus/Aunt Jemima, these conditions are crystal clear: the memes emerge not as description of persons of this kind or in an attempt to create or determine them but in an effort to defend a southern way of life wherein consensual Black subserviency "went without saying." The memes functioned, in other words, to represent Jim Crow as a positive good. That they appeared so often and in such neat alignment with the rise the segregation order suggests that the organicism required constant maintenance.

Still, the fantasy proved persuasive, and not only to southerners. Aunt Jemima became one the most successful brands of the twentieth century, and in James Webb Young and N. C. Wyeth's advertising campaign of the 1920s, she assembled an archive of Dixie memes. Her cabin, one ad proclaimed, "became more famous than Uncle Tom's," and her residence at the Louisiana plantation of Colonel Higbee, where "guests dropped in to stay a week or two," saw her assume the burden of southern hospitality.[159] In one ad she saves the colonel's reputation as host by providing breakfast when her mother takes a "mis'ry'; in another, she rescues two Confederate soldiers from Yankee capture, a storyline revisited in a later ad in which the one of the soldiers returns twenty years later on the riverboat *Rob't E. Lee* to visit her cabin, taking with him a "representative of a large flour mill" who purchases her recipe for pancake mix.[160] Receiving the "highest Medal" at the 1893 World's Fair, she "thought not so much of it as of the kind words her old 'massa' had spoken to her years and years before, his simpler words of appreciation for her loyalty and cheerful service."[161] As Karen Cox argues in *Dreaming of Dixie*, industries outside the South made liberal use of "the idyllic images conjured up by the Old South," exerting, through advertisements, radio, movies, and other media, "more influence over what ideas Americans consumed about the South than did native southerners themselves."[162] Nor did the memes of Dixie remain south of the Canadian border: songwriter Raymond B. Egan of Ontario, more famous for "Ain't We Got Fun," chimed in with "They Made It Twice as Nice as Paradise: And They Called it Dixieland," which recalls a "dear old Mammy" who "used to cuddle me upon her knee."[163]

But what proved attractive to outsiders was urgent to the kind of southerner described by T. Harry Williams: a fellow "marvelously adept at creating mind-pictures of his world or of the larger world around him—images that he wants to believe, that are real to him and that he will insist others accept."[164] Through compulsive iteration and the magic of anamorphosis, the distortion seemed real. And so we find Donald Davidson in the course of reviewing John Dollard's 1937 book *Class and Caste in a Southern Town* experiencing a kind of vertigo. "The perspective has altered sickeningly," he reports. "All that was big has become little. All that was little has swelled up fantastically." Anchoring his vision in a mind picture of his Black cook, he finds it "a comfort to think of Chloe as a reality" impervious to Dollard's distortion. "It is a little hard," Davidson writes, "for a Southern-towner to get Dr. Dollard's notion straight in his head." Even so, he tries: "The whole thing is, he says, an enormous conspiracy of the dominant whites to keep themselves in the relative position they enjoyed when whites were masters and the Negroes were slaves. White society, we must understand, is organized around a fiction which establishes whites as the superior caste and Negroes as the inferior caste." For Davidson, by contrast, the "bi-racial arrangement is firmly established" and "very familiar." Indeed, it had "been fairly well accepted as a *modus vivendi* for some centuries"—at least until Dollard arrived, perspective in hand, to "prove that things are not what they seem."[165]

In the aftermath of the civil rights movement, it's Davidson's modus vivendi that looks like the conspiracy theory. When I teach this essay, my students have difficulty grasping Davidson's mind picture of the world—how he *can't* see that the Southerntown way of life isn't, at its core, a white supremacist project. But they know what Southerntown looks like: a small town—a *community*—with unlocked doors, a slower pace of life, and a unique sense of place. For some of them, it looks like Mayberry, which looks, incidentally, like what the Old South looked like to Davidson. As Allen Tate wryly puts it, Davidson imagined "a South without plantations raising cotton for export. That how he freed the slaves."[166] But most of them are aware of Mayberry's whiteness and for them, Southerntown—and indeed, the South—includes African Americans among the group, as having belonged to the group all along. In my next chapter, I suggest that even this revised and reconstructed South is a bad idea.

CHAPTER 3

The South
Is a Bad Idea

In a 1955 speech delivered in Memphis, Senator James O. Eastland of Mississippi declares that, in the battle over segregation, "defeat means death, the death of Southern culture and our aspirations as an Anglo-Saxon people. Generations of southerners yet unborn will cherish our memory because they will realize that the fight we now wage will have preserved for them their untainted racial heritage, their culture and the institutions of the Anglo-Saxon race." Like Calhoun in his defense of slavery, Eastland argues not merely on behalf of an institution but on behalf of a people. That southerners were an Anglo-Saxon people nearly went without saying, having been said so often and for so long. (Few recalled that southerners had once been a Norman people.) But "Anglo-Saxon" also served, as it long had, as a mediating term between South and nation, a way for Eastland to imagine alliances in what he characterizes as a "crusade to restore Americanism" that would "carry on its banner the slogan of free enterprise."[1] This was a somewhat crude effort to align the South and American capitalism against the communist menace, Cold War politics in the developing world having rendered segregation a national burden.

In yoking the fate of a people to another peculiar institution, Eastland proved doubly wrong. In the space of a generation, Jim Crow went from appearing distinctive, organic, and foundational to appearing as slavery had: an embarrassment southerners came quickly to disavow. In 1962, George Wallace spoke from "the very Heart of the Great Anglo-Saxon Southland" and "in the name of the greatest people that have ever trod this earth" to declare "segregation now . . . segregation tomorrow . . . segregation forever."[2] In real time, "forever" turned out to be a matter of years, after which the foundational nature of segregation to the "southern way of life" was quickly forgotten. But for the signatories of the 1956 Southern Manifesto, including the entire congressional delegations of seven Confederate states, the Plessy decision had "became a part of the life of the people of many of the states and confirmed their habits, traditions, and way of life." As during the "War of Northern Aggression" (a recent coinage), "agitators and troublemakers invading our States" threatened to "destroy the amicable relations between the white and Negro races" made possible by the doctrine of separate but equal.[3] Drawing deep from the well of Dixie memes—Anglo Saxonism! localism! tradition! Northern Aggression! the close relation of races separated by law!—the defense of segregation was rendered as an inevitable and organic expression of the southern people.

But if Eastland was wrong about how "generations of Southerners yet unborn" would remember him, he was also wrong to equate the end of Jim Crow with the "death of Southern culture." Ostensibly detached from the Anglo-Saxon race, the notional South flourished as a multiracial culture and, eventually, a multicultural one, resulting in the decline of many Dixie memes, especially those rooted in blood. "Southern people" now takes the plural verb, and few of them imagine the group as having an Anglo-Saxon or Cavalier lineage. Others survived, and most mutated. The battle flag of the Army of Northern Virginia, having been deployed as an instrument of lost cause remembrance by the United Daughters of the Confederacy and various veteran's organizations, evolved into an explicit symbol of the segregationist movement, first appearing in this role at the Dixiecrat Convention of 1948. In 1956, it would appear in the state flag of Georgia, where it would remain until 2003. In 2020, Mississippi became the last state to remove the image of what is widely known as the "Confederate" or "rebel" flag. That same year, a Quinnipiac poll showed that, for the first time, a majority of southerners (55 percent), associated the flag with racism, while only 36 percent viewed it as a symbol of southern pride.[4]

Even for that 36 percent, however, "southern pride" means something different from segregation, hence the dissociation of heritage from hate in the bumper sticker everyone knows. The flag's clear and explicit association with the prosegregation movement likely doomed it in the long run, but it's worth noting that, for a time, it mutated to represent something like a heritage of abstract rebelliousness—the kind of thing practiced by, say, two good ole boys "fighting the system like two modern-day Robin Hoods," as the theme song from the *Dukes of Hazzard* has it. That mutation was, for a time, wildly successful, and not only in the Dukes of Hazzard franchise, where it replicated across millions of T-shirts, lunch boxes, and Hot Wheels versions of the General Lee. In music, the Confederate Chic movement of the 1960s and 1970s included figures on the left such as Ry Cooder ("I'm a Good Ole Rebel") and Joan Baez ("The Night They Drove Old Dixie Down"), while a host of fictional former Confederates—Shane, Rooster Cogburn, Josey Wales—would move to the West and the western to continue their fights against the system. To offer an analogy familiar in the age of COVID, one way viruses survive is by mutating to a less virulent or costly form. Arguably, the memic evolution of the flag was trending in this direction before its more recent attachment to an explicit politics of white nationalism. With this later mutation came greater copy fidelity—today, replication signifies something more specific than "rebelliousness"—and lower fecundity, since replication entails a higher social cost. When even Walmart refuses sell the flag, it's a bad idea to display it while applying for a job there, much less during an interview for a college scholarship. At the same time, increased virulence may enhance the meme's long-term survival because it is more important to the group it forms, which will, in turn, reproduce it with greater fervor.

My focus in this chapter, however, is not on the Confederate flag as currently construed or on the groups that it continues to form. Rather, I am interested in the memes of Dixie as they survived and mutated to reconstitute the southern group on a basis other than white supremacy—memes like the Confederate flag *if* it had continued to reproduce as a signifier of apolitical rebelliousness or *if* its NuSouth variant, which rendered the flag in "African" colors of red, green, and black, had outcompeted and supplanted its red, white, and blue ancestor.

As they evolved in the aftermath of the civil rights movement, the memes of Dixie continued to render the South axiomatic, a commonsense proposition that, as Cash famously puts it, only a journalist or professor would question.[5] I have argued, to the contrary, that we should think about the South not from the ground up but from the meme down—that is, from a close consideration of the replicated units through which groups have assembled under the banner of southernness and without assuming that those units emerge from a shared domain of what-goes-without-saying. Trying to extract a South from the ground up, always a difficult task, has, by any measure, proven more difficult with the decline of economic distinctiveness and the passing of peculiar institutions southerners once insisted were foundational. As Johnny Mercer puts it in his 1936 hit, "the famous old plantation has become a filling station / Dixie isn't Dixie anymore." For Mercer, of course, it was still Dixie because he continued to call it that and because not being what it was is Dixie's default condition.

But what happens when "Dixie" itself verges on extinction? The long decline of the term, first observed by John Shelton Reed and updated by Christopher A. Cooper and H.

Gibbs Knotts, has intensified of late.[6] The Dixie Chicks, who retained the "Dixie" while vocally opposing the Iraq war in 2003, dropped it in 2020, as did Dixie Beer a year later. According to general manager Jim Birch, "Community is at the heart of why we do what we do, and we thrive on the idea of our beer bringing people together. Our name must speak to the diversity of the city we call home as we encourage unity and inclusivity in New Orleans and across the country."[7] With Civil War monuments disappearing, the de-Confederationization of the South proceeds apace. If the group formerly known as Lady Antebellum is any indication, even the word "antebellum" is suspect. In 2020, it renamed itself Lady A, announcing in an Instagram post that "blindspots we didn't even know existed have been revealed." Although that's the nature of blind spots, the band's revelation is no less cloudy: "When we set out together almost 14 years ago, we named our band after the southern 'antebellum' style home where we took our first photos. As musicians, it reminded us of all the music born in the south that influenced us . . . Southern Rock, Blues, R&B, Gospel and of course Country. But we are regretful and embarrassed to say that we did not take into account the associations that weigh down this word referring to the period of history before The Civil War, which includes slavery."[8] Why you'd associate the plantation house with blues, R&B, or southern rock is at least as curious as why you wouldn't associate it with slavery, but the motive for doing so seems clear: to preserve the "southernness" of the brand without weighing it down with the burden of slavery.

Still, and anachronism aside (the "antebellum" period obviously included slavery and didn't include R&B), I take Lady A at its word because, for one thing, I grew up in a neighborhood called Plantation Estates, and I didn't associate "plantation" with plantations, much less with slavery. As I've argued, memes rarely offer a clear picture, but they're good at producing blind spots and distortions. To make slavery look like a plantation requires certain things to be seen from a certain vantage or to be hidden from view altogether. What interests me is whether Lady A, in distancing itself from the untoward associations of "the period of history before The Civil War," continues to cite plantation memes that once assembled a slaveholding people. Is the A, in other words, acting as a zombie meme, an undead idea that continues to generate longing under a guise of disavowal?

I think so. The persistence of plantation memes was brought home to me early in this project when I asked my daughter, then in high school, what first came to mind when she thought of the South. Her answer, I think verbatim, was this: "a house like Monticello, with a big front porch and sweet tea," although she was quick to add, "on a good day." On a bad day, and I've heard her say such things frequently, the South is Confederate flag–waving Trump supporters. So I was a little surprised to hear Monticello, and a little sorry to hear that for her, as for many, the South still looks like a plantation, at least "on a good day." These, then, constitute the memes to which I direct my attention: items such as plantations, front porches, and sweet tea that have remained or become southern and that continue to assemble groups calling themselves southerners.

Although I return momentarily to the ascent of "culture" as what defines southernernness, let me offer a few generalizations about the mutation patterns of southern memes in the aftermath of the civil rights movement. First, as we've seen, many of them actively disavow connections to Dixie. In a now paradigmatic founding act, *Bitter Southerner*, bitter over (among other things) the South's status as a "national laughing stock" due to conclusions "folks" draw from southerners "hopelessly bound to tradition," assembles a group of "Southern people who do cool things, smart things" and "honor genuinely honorable traditions." In the inclusive South of "All Y'all" (as one of the group's T-shirt has it), those who "fly the rebel flag" or "think women look really nice in hoop skirts" are politely asked to excuse themselves. Second, many of these memes are apparently novel. Although *Bitter Southerner* sells a T-shirt that reads "mayo and tomato" that "declares any good Southerner's allegiance" to the sandwich, neither John C. Calhoun nor George Wallace thought to reference cuisine in constructing a South to which allegiance was due.[9]

Third, many memes survive as apparently benign mutations of older memes. In a 2022 article titled "Southern Traditions We Want to Bring Back—And You Will Too," *Southern Living* includes, predictably, southern hospitality, the "genuine" version of which, we are told, "means an open-door policy to family, neighbors, co-workers, friends, friends of friends, and even friendly strangers. While times have changed enough that you need to trust your instincts, generally, when someone shows up on your porch, greet them with a smile and maybe a glass of sweet tea."[10] (More genuineness, porches, and sweet tea.) Although this variant of southern hospitality is far removed from the defense of a slaveholding people, it is, as Anthony Szczesiul demonstrates in *The Southern Hospitality Myth*, clearly continuous with that idea.

Fourth, the group boundary expanded to include persons of color. This proved conceptually challenging, since the identitarian South had, from its inception, been founded in the defense of slavery and, later, Jim Crow. For W. J. Cash, the many Souths converged into one through "a complex of established relationships and habits of thought, sentiments, prejudices, standards and values, and associations of ideas, which, if it is not common strictly to every group of *white people in the South*, is still common in one appreciable measure or other, and in some part or another, to all but relatively negligible ones."[11] The savage ideal, "whereunder . . . men become in all their attitudes, professions, and actions, virtual replicas of one another," extended only to white minds and, for Cash, obviously so. Similarly, Ulrich B. Phillips identifies white supremacy as the "cardinal test of a Southerner" and "the central theme of Southern history" and found it unnecessary to clarify that he was talking about the *white* South.[12] Writing in 1933, Allen Tate insists that when "radically different races live together, one must rule," and the situation would not change even "had we a superior race like the Chinese in our midst."[13] According to Mark Malvasi, Tate embraced this view "in defense of the South's community and culture, which he believed would not survive without the stern imposition of racial homogeneity."[14] An integrated South, Tate notes in 1962, "would not be my world."[15]

Once integrated, however, the South remained southern, and its racial homogeneity was found to be in error. According to Eugene Genovese, Tate's mistake was not that he proffered a "tribal argument of us against them." In Genovese's view, tribal arguments are fine, since "without a large measure of cultural homogeneity no community could expect to survive, much less thrive." Rather, Tate had identified the wrong "us," having "woefully underestimated the 'southernness' of southern blacks and their contributions to the regional culture."[16] For Genovese, then, Tate's error was to think of Black persons in the Southeast as though they were like the Chinese (racially *and* culturally different), when in fact they were cultural southerners all along.

And so the southern way of life that had sanctioned racial segregation was retconned to show that the culture had been biracial (at least) all along, thus avoiding much of the burden of southern history and also the awkwardness of a cultural heritage dating only to the 1960s. The adjustment involved reassigning memes across the color line. In southern literary studies, Fred Hobson argues in his 1992 Lamar Lectures that "the black Southerner" might be seen not just, as C. Vann Woodward had argued, as the quintessential southerner or the quintessential southern agrarian but "the quintessential southern writer—with his emphasis on family and community, his essentially concrete vision, his feeling for place, *his* legacy of failure, poverty, defeat, and those other well-known qualities of the southern experience, *his* immersion in history and what it produced."[17] Those "well-known qualities" suggest that memes are in play, but the italics—*his*, the black southerner's—indicate, like Genovese's scare-quoted "southernness," that a mutation has occurred, at least for the purposes of Team Southern Writers. Soon, it would become clear that Richard Wright was a southern writer and always had been, despite rarely being described as such during his lifetime. Within a quarter century, it would be evident to Cooper and Knotts that "Black southerners have no doubt always considered themselves southerners," despite the lack of any evidence supporting the claim and their observation a few pages later that "the traditional role of racism in southern identity also excluded African Americans, a group that made up a substantial portion of the southern population."[18]

Because of their nebulous nature, memes proved essential in the retroactive integration of southern culture. If "southern culture" no longer belonged to a race (as it did for Eastland), an alternative anchor could be found in place. In *The Encyclopedia of Southern Culture*'s "Place, Sense of" entry, Charles Reagan Wilson provides, as part of the "extensive" "evidence for a deep-seated southern sense of place," the alleged fact that "the first settlers in the region, Native Americans, saw the Lands of the Southeast as sacred ground, with all happenings in their specific places related to the rest of the cosmos." Precisely what claim is being made here is far from clear. That the "Lands of the Southeast" have always generated sacred attachments? That the Native American sense of place was passed on to the settler colonists who displaced them? The motive, however, seems evident. Like Lady A dissociating the plantation house from slavery and reattaching it to blues and R&B, Wilson detaches "place" from its traditional associations—recall that he's reminded us that "until recently southern whites frequently used place to indicate the status of blacks"—and rendered it the possession of all. But what other "extensive evidence" supports the claim? Wilson cites Eudora Welty, who says nothing about a *southern* sense of place, but does say that "*feelings* are bound up in place," which is probably true. Then Wilson quotes Reed, "who has concluded that 'southerners seem more likely than other Americans to think of their region, their states, and their local communities as theirs, and as distinct from and preferable to other regions, states, and localities.'"[19] That's a quotation from *The Enduring South*, where Reed also concedes that the "evidence for Southern localism is not as clearcut as we might wish." "Seem" and "wish" tell us a group trait is being revealed, against the author's wishes, as a statistical variation. According to the three polls Reed cites (conducted in 1939, 1944, and 1963), southerners prefer living in their home state more than aggregated nonsoutherners—by percentages of 8, 9, and 7. In every poll, they trail residents of the Pacific states, including California, not known for its localism. Shifting from profession to practice, Reed concludes that "although census data show Southerners to be about as likely as any other Americans to leave their home state and region, there is abundant qualitative evidence from every jukebox that they are much more likely to complain about having left."[20]

That's a great line and an even more important point. It is precisely because group identities are based on difference, not on evidence or statistical variation, that we are more likely to encounter the South on a jukebox than in Nashville, on reality television than on the local news, or in *Southern Living* than in southeastern life. We know what Lady A's "southern 'antebellum' style home" looks like because it appears in every film, not because it looks like most houses on prewar plantations. In literature, the South is most likely to appear in that most trope-laden of genres, the "southern gothic." In imagining "a highly successful series of hack 'southern' detective novels," Jon Smith hits most of the tropes:

> In each, a child—a Jem or Scout or Frankie or Richard or Opie—is eating a MoonPie or drinking an RC Cola, walking barefoot, feeling the warm red summer clay of the fields between her or his toes. But what's this lying in the brush, at the bottom of the catfish pond, protruding from behind the springhouse? It's a scrap of fabric, the child tugs, it turns out to reveal a long-decomposed body. A black man who disappeared years ago, a black woman who must have been, just must have been, someone's mistress. The detective—an updated Gavin Stevens type or a Rita Mae Brown protagonist with a cat, it doesn't matter—is called to the scene, investigates. Old Dark Secrets

are uncovered. Black families and white families turn out to be related. Money changed hands, or didn't. Someone white and powerful—a judge, a preacher, in every fourth volume a congressman—tries to halt the investigation. A black preacher discovers in a trunk a cache of old photos (what are *those* two doing in the same picture, smiling?), a journal (it doesn't spell things out, but just complicates things more!), an enigmatic doll that may be a clue. In the end, a measure of justice is accomplished, the community is reunited, but reminded of the presence of the past.[21]

Because the southern way of life has always differed from the southeastern way of living, the memes of Dixies have long flourished in symbolic environments.[22]

But even there, southern difference can prove elusive. If Welty was unconcerned with a southern sense of place, Brad Watson finds, for the umpteenth time, that it's the "most distinctive" thing about southern literature. Of course there are the usual caveats: with hundreds of writers, the "work can be quite varied in quite various ways"; the South itself, being "actually a large part of this country," comprises many and varied subregions, including "of course the Mississippi Delta, which ought to be considered a discrete Southern region all its own." But out of the welter of the southern pluribus comes "sense of place" to recover the unum, as evidenced by the "junkyard in James L. Dickey's 'Cherrylog Road,'" which, he maintains, is different, "with its curling vines and sexually charged, high-humidity heat, from just any old American junkyard," such as those in New Jersey or Watson's "current home of Laramie, Wyoming." Then, too, the "bayous in James Lee Burke's Robicheaux novels are quite distinctive from a New England marsh . . . or a man-made swimming hole in Texas." Finally, eccentric characters in the stories of George Singleton are said to be more likely to encounter stray dogs than similar characters in the stories of T. C. Boyle. This is far from a QED-type situation. Note that in two instances, literary landscapes are compared with geographical ones, as though the southern poem (or a highly successful series of detective novels) is climactically determined by, among other things, heat and humidity. Note also that the literary bayou in Louisiana differs not only from an actual New England marsh but also from a swimming hole in Texas and, presumably, a pocosin in North Carolina. Are we to imagine that the pocosin, because it is in the South, would produce a distinctive sense of place like that of the bayou (if someone like James Lee Burke were to write a highly successful series of detective novels about it), but that the marsh wouldn't? Not necessarily, because, according to Watson, "a sense of place in fiction is just as important in one piece of fiction, set anywhere, . . . as it is in the South." But the South "is actually still distinctive from other regions. As they are distinctive from the South."[23] Thus, a truism—that any bounded region of the earth, from a front yard to a continent, is distinctive from any other— is transformed, somehow, into a distinctive property of the South such that a distinctive literature will continue to grow from the ground up.

This raises the question I posed at the art exhibit I mentioned in the introduction: what is this *South* that includes North Carolina and Louisiana, despite their differing wetlands, but not New England and (possibly?) Texas? What *one* South binds the former and excludes the latter? For Donald Davidson, identifying Southerntown was easy: it was the town—all towns—where the biracial modus vivendi was under attack from Yankee outsiders. But what happens when, as Arjun Appadurai says, *what* southern locality is produced "against, in spite of, and in relation to" *isn't* abolitionists threatening to provoke race insurrection, Union armies threatening southern firesides, carpetbaggers imposing "negro rule," Darwinists attacking the old-time religion, or "agitators and troublemakers invading our States" to impose equality before the law? How does place, long associated with those contexts and projects, continue to support the notion of southern difference? When heat is embedded in an argument about slavery, it's obvious why the South, even the cooler parts of it, must be distinctively hot. How does it continue to define a South when that argument is over?

Pretty easily, in fact. I'll eventually get around to arguing that the argument isn't over, but for now, let me reiterate that what's important about memes is not that they're true but that they generate belief and believers. They function as the basis of, as Kwame Anthony Appiah argues, an identity that people assume "survives through time and space" because it is "underwritten by some larger, shared commonality; an essence that all the instances share."[24] Apparently, "sense of place" has accumulated enough ibidinal intensity to compel citation by the minds—in the cases of Hobson, Reed, and Wilson, first-rate minds—that hold it. One senses in the examples I've cited an effort to protect the meme from rational analysis, to find some—*any*—evidence of a shared commonality, even if it means relying on a jukebox rather than a poll.

Motivated reasoning is evident in every effort to rationalize the multiSouth—that is, the existence of one South comprising many. In dividing the South into thirds, Hugh Holman concedes that he is "oversimplifying a very complex geographical, historical, and social pattern" but insists that the oversimplification "serves as a corrective for a larger oversimplification which has commonly been made."[25] But if the new map is also oversimplified, why stop at three? Why not carve out New Orleans from the Deep South, or Appalachia from the mountain and Piedmont South, or James Dickey's junkyard from that other junkyard a county over? More importantly, if the lesser simplifications are more geographically specific, such that a culture can appear to arise more plausibly from the ground up, why continue to house them in the larger one? Any ontological conception of southern cultures runs into this problem: for the cultures to be southern, either there must be a quantum of southernness possessed by all of the cultures—a "larger, shared commonality"—or "southern" is merely designating their location. But if the South is just an address—if it's just the Southeast—it's no longer a culture, at least if culture has anything to do with group identity.

Addressing the problem from an ostensibly postontological vantage, Richard Gray claims that "the South is an imagined community made up of a multiplicity of communities, similarly imagined." But to ensure that the many imagined communities aren't all just *located* in the southern one (otherwise the southern one wouldn't be an imagined community), Gray needs, and purports to find, a shared commonality. What fuses the many into the one, he claims, is that they "share . . . the need to make a place in the world with the aid of talk and ceremony, language and communal ritual." Gray concedes that this is a "human need" and thus not a distinctively southern one, so he adds that "less abstractly, it is something that drives southerners to position themselves *with* others in their locality, communality of interest, or area, and *against* or *apart from* others elsewhere."[26] Yet since this is also universally true, it remains unclear how two contending localities in, say, Arkansas, would both be southern or what they would share categorically with the locality of Charleston, where communalities of interest may differ even within the city limits. Absent an ontological basis, there is simply no way to meaningfully collate the smaller imagined communities into the larger one unless some variant of "the North" continues to function as what southerners position themselves *against* or *apart from*. In a similar attempt to grow the region from the ground up, Wendell Berry denounces the "spurious piety" often associated with "Southern regionalism," advocating instead a "regionalism . . . defined simply *as local life aware of itself*."[27] But how much of the region can a local truly be aware of? And how is awareness of *local* life somehow *regional* in nature?

I've argued that the South has never emerged organically from an actual way of living or actual places but rather from identitarian disputation against an equally imagined region called the North. (If you're a southerner whose thinks of midwesterners, not Yankees, as the kind of person from which you're fundamentally different, you're disproving my point.) As an imagined community, it has developed banners to rally around, one of them being locality—of having a distinctive and unique sense of place. These memes (including "community") have served as figments of imagined community, and successfully so, compelling citation and replication, ensuring legibility, and constituting self-evidence. Today, a period in which many southerners report being able to see the local from their house, everyone knows about southern culture and its distinctive sense of place, but no one has heard of Georgian culture or the Memphian sense of place. Few identify, in the terms of Holman's trinitarian South, as Tidewaterians, Piedmontians, or deep southerners.

Put another way, the South needs locality more than vice versa, since if the distinctive *sense* derived from actual *places*—that is, if it were determined by climate and geography or even Reed's "climates" of demography and preidentitarian "culture"—we wouldn't end up with a South shaped like the Confederate States of America. But that's pretty much what the South is shaped like, give or take south Florida, Missouri, and a few other disputed regions. The *Bitter Southerner* once offered a "South without Borders" T-shirt, which showed the border of "the whole South, with no boundaries inside it." "We like that idea," its editors explained, the idea of "one big region that soaks up the power of every one of the hundreds of cultures inside it."[28] Liking the idea is as good an explanation as you'll find. What idea is being liked, however, isn't clear from the shirt itself, which, as Margaret McGehee observes, "clearly depicts a bordered and bounded region" lacking cultural subdivision and possibly including "cultures" wherein hoop skirts are considered acceptable garb.[29] Minus the explanation, the T-shirt looks a lot like the Confederacy, which probably explains why it was discontinued. As Michael O'Brien pithily observes, "the search for Southern distinctiveness is a logical nightmare," while "in the search for Southern identity wishes are overmastering."[30]

One reason the South is still shaped like the Confederate States of America is that many of the memes most useful in imagining *the earlier* imagined community—one amounting to an actual nation, not just a nation within a nation, or the next thing to it, or a "culture"—have survived to keep the southern group together. How, then, have the memes of a slaveholding people evolved to accommodate the progressive multitude? With Dixie disavowed and with the group now excluding the oaf flying his Confederate flag, what banners continue to persuade individuals not only to believe in the South but to belong to it? If "Dixie is dead," as Tracy Thompson proclaims in the *Bitter Southerner*, what remains of the South? For Thompson, it turns out to be quite a lot. After the usual round of the usual caveats—stronger and more powerful "tribal affiliations" are forming; there is an increasing "number of various immigrant groups"; the region, "just as in the rest of the country," now comprises "balkanized communities"—Thompson begins with "a single premise: The South is where the red dirt is." This is a novel effort to build the South from the ground up, since her red dirt remains geological rather than morphing into an essentialized "soil"— the kind of "beautiful red earth," for example, so admired by Katie Scarlett and her father. But the premise doesn't work very well in creating a South: the Mississippi Delta lacks red dirt but is "included" for reasons unexplained, as is western Pennsylvania, "which is red dirt [and] is also included because in cultural terms its basically an extension of Appalachia." Thus Appalachia, suddenly lacking in balkanized communities, shares "cultural terms" with, apparently, the Mississippi Delta and part of a state that trailed only New York in supplying Union soldiers.

Red dirt not having settled anything, Thompson moves to more promising ground: Reed's research comparing the use of "Dixie" and "southern" in the names of businesses. You may recall that Albion Tourgée similarly identified the "mystically-bounded" South as the place where "the word 'Southern' leaps into prominence" in branding things "as distinctively and specifically 'Southern.'" Reed's data-driven confirmation of Tourgée's insight tells us *where* southerners are in precisely the way that a hypothetical poll might show that Atlanta Braves fans are concentrated in Georgia. But it doesn't tell us what makes a southerner into a *kind of person* unless it is telling us exactly what the poll is telling us—that is, the location of persons who support Team South or who, like Louis Rubin, believe that "southern identity is important because it is."

Having insisted that the South isn't Dixie and that it's not just the tribalized, balkanized, politically divided Southeast, Thompson must, and does, locate a common denominator. What connects her, an anti-Obama fanatic she had unfriended on Facebook, and Patrice, a Black friend "who lives in an otherwise all-white gated community in South Carolina"? All claim to be southerners. But

> What is it we are all claiming? An accent? A shared taste for hominy grits? The accident of being born at a certain latitude and longitude?
>
> I think it's more: I think the tap root is memory.
>
> . . .
>
> History happened to *us*. It either happened to us personally, as some who were on the Edmund Pettus Bridge that day in Selma can attest, or to our direct ancestors, or (in my case) right across the street from the house where I grew up, where Sherman's soldiers tore up the railroad one day in August 1864 (he describes the location very precisely in his memoirs).[31]

But if, as she's already noted, what happened on the bridge demonstrates that "Southerners are more than capable of expressing their political differences by beating the shit out [of] each other," then where's the southern *us*? To whom did that event happen, personally or otherwise? Did it happen equally to the marchers and the Confederate flag wavers at the other end of the bridge? Did it happen to persons living in the Southeast today—probably a majority—who don't know what happened on the bridge? And if *us* constitutes the group whose railroad tracks were torn up by Sherman, does that group include Hispanic immigrants who lack "direct ancestors" in the Southeast, don't live across the street from the railroad tracks he destroyed, and indeed may not have heard of Sherman? Does it include Patrice? As always, the shared commonality deteriorates under scrutiny.

In a way, of course, Thompson is right: to the extent that

history happened to us, it constitutes us. But that is very different from history understood as simply what happened or from a self-evident understanding of who we are in which it's clear which history happened to us and which happened to other people. As Ernst Renan pointed out a century and a half ago, history only works that way if it's edited and reiterated enough to sustain the daily plebiscite through which the nation reproduces.[32] But it's worth considering whether, if what we're claiming as the basis of our identity is what Sherman did to us or what (more passively) happened to us through Sherman, the group identity is worth preserving. If the railroad tracks have been repaired—surely they have—is it time to retire the Sherman meme? If not, is Dixie really dead?

Reconsidering the MoonPie

In an essay I published about a decade ago, I mentioned offhandedly that I considered the South to be mostly a bad idea.[33] By this, I meant at least two things. First, I meant that the South was a poor analytical category to use in understanding the region and nation—that it included too many mythologies that distorted realities; that it promised cultural coherence in what amounted to subregionally differentiated and internally balkanized communities; that it purported to explain phenomena better explained through other analytical categories (economic class, race, political affiliation, population density, and so forth); that it imagined the southerner to be a *kind* of person and a southern novel to be a *kind* of novel, which I doubted. Second, I meant that the idea of a distinctive southern people, civilization, and culture had, all things considered, done more harm than good. But I also argued in the essay that the idea of the South had improved considerably. If the MoonPie, as William Ferris has claimed, had come to anchor southerners in "their history and culture," better the MoonPie than a statue of Nathan Bedford Forrest. And if the MoonPie, which, according to the marketing for it, is a "southern thing" that "you wouldn't understand," better the MoonPie than other southern things (slavery and segregation, for instance) that outsiders had long been deemed incapable of understanding. And so, I concluded that a South built of food memes—I'm sorry, *foodways*—was a bit fraudulent but, on the whole, unobjectionable. Better pledging your allegiance to the 'mater sandwich, as any good southerner is obliged to do, than to the Confederate flag.

As I've mentioned in passing, this was an easy conclusion for me to reach because not having much of one, southern identity doesn't strike me as very important. One reason for this, I think, is that my early encounters with many "southern things" was ambivalent or unmarked. I had no idea that the MoonPie was even conceivably a southern thing until informed so by a grad school professor from New England. My family ate turnip greens, black-eyed peas, and cornbread on New Year's Day, but I was unaware that this was a "southern tradition." I didn't especially like any of these foods, and I especially disliked grits, which, because I was always slow to the breakfast table, I generally ate cold and alongside a slice or two of Sizzlean, a pseudobacon since consigned to the dustbin of gastronomic history. I did know that grits (and iced tea) were southern because Lewis Grizzard, a columnist at the *Atlanta Journal-Constitution*, was always banging on about them. A column republished by the paper in a 2019 retrospective will give you a taste of his style:

> Cherokee Indians, native to the Southern region of the United States, first discovered grits trees growing wild during the 13th century. Chief Big Bear's (wife), Jemima Big Bear, is said to have been out of oatmeal one day, so she gathered the tiny grits growing from the grits trees and cooked them in water for Chief Big Bear.
>
> After eating the grits, Chief Big Bear ordered his (wife), Jemima, burned at the stake.
>
> Later, however, Southern planter Jim Dandy found grits taste a lot better if you put salt and pepper and butter on them. Grits really took off in the South after that.[34]

I'm not sure I would have been offended by the column if I had read it when it originally appeared in 1980 (I don't think I did), but I'm sure I wouldn't have found it funny. This is the South as schtick, the South of *Hee Haw* (also not funny), *Gomer Pyle* (mildly funny), and *The Beverly Hillbillies* (funny); no one really lived there. And so lacking a taste for grits, I also lacked a shared taste for them—that is, the idea that a love of grits connected me with strangers in Alabama and separated me from strangers in Illinois. Southerness, simply, was a voluntary matter, a group you could join by adopting its symbols, dress, musical preferences, and the like as you might choose to become a punk or a preppy. It was a style, a performance.

While I found Grizzard's performance annoying at the time, I likely missed what seems obvious in rereading his work. First, there is a deep antagonism toward "folks from New Jersey and places like that" (the stated audience for his "guide to a southern delicacy"). Possibly this derived from his three years of "exile"—his word—in Chicago, which he documented in a book whose gist is clear from its title: *If I Ever Get to Georgia, I'm Gonna Nail My Feet to the Ground*. Before and during his move to Chicago, Grizzard was a sportswriter; when he returned, he became, professionally, a southerner. (In the interim, he was accused of racism by a sportswriter named Lacy Banks, whose subsequent firing was later overturned by a federal arbitrator.) Second, there is the overt and offensive stereotyping. Of course the name of the cartoonish Cherokee "(wife)" had to be Jemima; in the original column, she had been Chief Big Bear's "squaw." Of course "Southern planter Jim Dandy" saves the day with salt, pepper, and butter, allowing grits to take off "in the South." This raises the question of whether grits as a novel meme differentiating southerners from folks from places like New Jersey is in fact a mutation of obsolescent memes functioning in an altered discursive context. If the planter answered the charge that southerners were slaveholders and if Aunt Jemima answered the charge that they were white supremacists, are grits answering the charge that southerners were, to use a term that gained broad traction in the 1960s, "racists"? In rendering grits as a cardinal test of a grit-eating people, is Grizzard tacitly responding to that lurking accusation?

I suspect so, which has led me to reevaluate the MoonPie and other adjacent memes. Certainly the interpellation—of being seen as "that kind" of southerner—has proven durable. "The South is racist" can be found in virtually any comments section wherein the South is debated, and when Seth Stephens-Davidowitz concludes as a result of his analysis of Google Trends data that "much of what we thought about the location of racism [in the U.S.] was wrong," what he's referencing by "what we thought" is the idea that racism is located in the South.[35] More recently, Imani Perry observes in *South to America* that "'racism,' despite all evidence of its ubiquity, is still commonly described as 'belonging' to the South," and she goes on to argue that "the consequence of the projection of national sins, and specifically racism, onto one region is a mis-narration of history and American identity."[36] This restates the argument of Marcus Anthony Hunter and Zandria Robinson in *Chocolate Cities*. While they acknowledge that the "accepted map of Black life in the United States" imagines the "Mason-Dixon line . . . [as] a mythical and actual barrier between freedom and enslavement, North and South, progressive race relations and Old South," they maintain that this is a mistake. Following Malcolm X's claim that "as long as you South of the Canadian border, you South," they identify "manufactured distinctions" between "the North" and "the South" such that all of the United States constitutes "versions" of "the South," including the Northeast ("Up South"), Midwest ("Mid South"), Southwest ("West South"), and Northwest ("Out South").[37] In both cases, however, the "projection" or "manufactured distinction" persists: for Hunter and Robinson, as for Malcolm X, all of the United States becomes "the South," while, according to the dust jacket of *South to America*, "if we want to build a more humane future for the United States, we must center our concern below the Mason-Dixon line."

As a practical matter, I suspect such a centering is unwise. A recent study from Berkeley's Othering and Belonging Institute concludes that "contrary to prevailing impressions of the United States, the most segregated regions are the Midwest and Mid-Atlantic, followed by the West Coast. Southern states have lower overall levels of racial residential segregation, and the Mountain West and Plains states have the least."[38] If residential segregation constitutes a form of structural racism, then why not address it where it exists rather than where prevailing impressions believe it does? For decades, studies have shown patterns of school and residential segregation with weak, nonexistent, or negative correlations to the Southeast; perhaps it's time to square the prevailing impressions with the data. The broad point, I think, is obvious: if "the South" is, as Hunter and Robinson suggest, a "shorthand for systematic inequality and racism," it's a relatively imprecise shorthand.[39]

Two points, however, complicate the claim. First, as I've argued throughout, shorthand is crucial to group formation. Writing for *Vox*, Jemar Tisby describes himself as "a black man who moved to the Deep South" and more specifically to the Mississippi Delta, a "region that brings up pictures of slavery, lynching, and poverty" and constitutes the "cradle of American racism." Writing for *Newsweek*, Charles Love, in describing a summer spent in Charleston, notes that "those of us who don't live in the South often talk about it as if the whole region is frozen in 1965 Selma." Tisby experiences residential segregation and concludes that "racism never really goes away. It just changes forms." Love finds, conversely, that "what they're telling you about racism there is wrong," reporting that "white and black Southerners treated me and everyone else with kindness and respect."[40] Despite their different findings (which may boil down to differences between the Mississippi Delta and Charleston or to differences in their individual experiences), both are traveling to the same imagined region—presumed enemy territory—and extrapolate from their experiences (a single summer, in Love's case) conclusions about an entire region. In addition, Tisby's South (but not Love's) isn't *just* enemy territory; it's also "our homeland away from home." It's "as close as many African Americans will get to their past," so much so, he insists, that "black folks . . . outside of this region" cannot "truly understand the nation or themselves unless they at least make a pilgrimage to the Deep South."[41] Whatever the sociological value of these very different conclusions, it is clear that the South continues to be useful—or at least to be used—in delineating group identities.

Second, claiming that racism isn't really a southern thing partakes in a long-standing practice of Dixie deflection and whattaboutism. Declarations of northern guilt have long functioned as protestations of southern innocence. A primary reason racism is understood as "belonging" to the South is that for centuries a condition of belonging to the South was the requirement that one defend peculiar institutions founded in racial inequity and oppression. If segregated schools existed not just in Montgomery, but Topeka, Kansas, no one in Topeka pronounced the *Brown* decision to herald the death of midwestern culture. And if residential segregation is higher in Milwaukee than in Atlanta (it is), no Wisconsonian ever denounced "agitators and troublemakers invading" the Cheese State. There are no northern variants of the southern traits mentioned on the back cover of *South to America*: "We all think we know the South. Even those who have never lived there can rattle off a list of signifiers: the Civil War, *Gone with the Wind*, the Ku Klux Klan, plantations, football, Jim Crow, slavery."

It's an interesting list, clearly intended for persons who have never lived there and probably written by one. The signifiers are racially loaded and, on balance, accusatory, collectively forming an interpellative framework crucial for understanding the development of the post–Jim Crow South. The anomalous term, perhaps, is "football," which appears, and probably because it is relatively free of racial baggage, to define the South in an early issue of *Southern Living* magazine. A year after the march on Edmund Pettus Bridge and five years after Bull Connor had denounced "these meddlers from out of our city" in the city where *Southern Living* is published, Romain Smith declares the South to be "football country" owing to "its teams and teamplay, its mild climate, and local social traditions."[42] Although the relationship between a mild climate and "football country" isn't obvious, football served as a reliable southern thing for the magazine, which named an all-South football team throughout the 1970s. Rebranding the South of Bull Connor as the South of football and azaleas was important to *Southern Living*'s postsegregation attempt at what Gina Caison, Stephanie Rountree, and Lisa Hinrichsen call regional remediation, wherein media "cycl[e] through iterations of mediated forms to attempt to remediate [the South's] image into something 'new.'"[43] In *Southern Living*'s inaugural issue, editor Eugene Butler explains that "the magazine you now hold will be truly Southern—edited for people living in the South," which he defines as "a part of the nation where emphasis is given to social, cultural, and recreational life." "This magazine," he assures readers, "is edited for the South's unique differences—its differences in geography and climate—in the way it works and lives—its differences in a hundred other ways," ways that go unnamed. He eagerly seeks "the friendship of such Southerners who take weekend trips, enjoy outdoor living—hunting, fishing, camping, boating—and are home owners." Missing in Butler's relentless tagging of things southern is any particular sense of what makes them so. Apart from its "mild climate," "uncrowded highways," and avoidance of "mistakes that have blighted so many Northern urban areas," the South appears nearly featureless and altogether lacking in differences perceived to be deficits.[44] Vanishingly rare is any mention of the "South many in the nation are led to *think* they see." That South, mentioned in passing by E. L. Holland, is an "archaic stereotype" perpetuated by writers like Erskine Caldwell who provide the unwitting consumer with "the South they'll 'buy.'" Contemporary writers were missing, Holland complains, the "bright modern South" where "'Tobacco Road' . . . is a controlled-access interstate." Possibly someone named Jeeter Lester lived in this world; if so, he was probably watching the Dallas Cowboys "from the box seats."[45]

Although the ghost of Caldwell's Jeeter Lester continues to shadow Holland's well-to-do Texan, it's a relatively mild form of haunting altogether free of the stigmata accumulated during a decade of civil rights conflict. In a typical story in *Southern Living*, a tour of Jackson, Mississippi, reveals a "city with a clean face and forward look." Not only was Jackson "the best educated city in the nation" boasting "a $13 million ultra-modern airport," but it also had a "day-lily bed 18,000 feet long" and a "talking garbage can" that scolded "any person [who] threw trash on the street."[46] In admonishing litterbugs, the garbage can addressed implicit accusations of southern squalor, but evaded entirely the charge that Medgar Evers had been murdered by a white supremacist. In whitewashing the South by representing it as free of racial conflict—indeed, nearly free of Black people—*Southern Living* exemplifies how, as Caison, Rountree, as Hinrichsen argue, the "the ever escaping promise of remediation" relapses into "re-mediation, where the mediated form only reproduces the problems that came before, just in a shiny new platform."[47] The shiny new platform was evident enough in a South made of new airports, azaleas, hunting, football, and, eventually, cast-iron cookware (although not yet; an article in the June 1966 issue trumpets the magic of Teflon). Attaching "southern" to these things cited and thus confirmed the existence of the "mystically bound region" to which they belonged. But within this ultrasunny South, the emergent lifestyle compulsively cited a long-standing way of life, re-mediating *through* many of older memes of Dixie. Atlanta is said to have a "nostalgic sense of Southern graciousness that sets her above other cities," but it's still the place where Sherman "wreaked . . . wholesale destruction."[48] Even as tourist attractions, Con-

federate monuments continue to anchor the South's historical geography, figuring prominently in a recurring feature
that asked readers to identify famous places in the South. The
blindingly white first volume of the magazine contains, apart
from a few musicians appearing in record ads, precisely two
images of Black persons. The first is Aunt Jemima, the second
a young waiter wearing a sandwich board menu at an Atlanta
restaurant called Aunt Fanny's Cabin. There, we learn, "until she was called to her reward at age 104, Aunt Fanny herself welcomed you into the old-timey house where she lived
as a slave girl. Now a Negro boy holding a lantern sings out,
'Welcome to Aunt Fanny's Cabin.'"[49] The new southern hospitality may feature casseroles and cookouts, but it also leans
on figures who are, or are very nearly, Aunt Jemima. As Amy
Elias notes, the undead uncle appears as late as 1995, when
a Hyatt ad featured a black "door captain" named Charlie
Ferguson rendering services "with a hospitality the South is
known for." As Elias shrewdly demonstrates in her analysis
of this and other images, "simulations of Old-South racial stereotypes" remained systematically "encoded in contemporary
vacation advertising for southern locations."[50] The Sun Belt
South, in other words, looked a lot like the Old South under
new management.

For Elias, a self-consciously managed and marketed South
marked a "new kind of postmodern hyperreality, one where
regional characteristics are logos to be put on T-shirts and
bumper stickers rather than something rooted in the real habits, manners, customs, and history of a geographical location."
In this new virtual environment, she argues, the issue is not so
much "whether the South *has* a regional distinctiveness" but
rather "who controls representation of regional characteristics, for what audiences, and with what objectives."[51] I was
sympathetic to this view, as I was to Griffin and Thompson's
conception of "symbolic southernness"—a group identity
no longer (but once!) "rooted in the routines of everyday life
or the attributions of nonsoutherners" and thus not requir-
ing "an actually existing distinctive South." But my sympa-

thy presupposed what this book has argued against: that the "real" habits, routines, customs, and so forth once existed in a kind of autochthonous enclave separate from the project of representing and controlling southern identity. There has only ever been symbolic southernness—that is, a group identity formed by rallying *against* the attributions of outsiders and *around* banners (or T-shirts) with logos ranging from "slavery as a positive good" and hospitality to Aunt Jemima and tomato sandwiches. These, in turn, have never been "rooted in" the everyday, except as defenses and distortions of what existed there.[52] Southerners have never been trees, although they have often thought themselves so. Simply put, there has never been an unmediated South, a South (consisting of things like regional characteristics, group traits, cultural habits, and the like) *prior to* contested representations of those things. If there had been, we would never have heard of it.

Back in the early 2000s, I would have argued further (and did to an extent) that the decay or liquidation of a self-evident and solid South meant the opportunity for negotiation and improvisation within and across group boundaries. Doesn't Alex Haley introduce *The Encyclopedia of Southern Culture* by asking if "you remember those southern elder men who 'jes set' on their favored chair or bench for hours, every day— and a year later they could tell you at about what time of time of day someone's dog had trotted by?" Of course I didn't then (and you don't now), but imagining our "southern ancestors, black and white" as "foundational timbers" supporting "'the southern way of life'" seemed preferable to the crooked timber from which the southern way of life had long been fashioned.[53] Then, too, there were other Black constructions of the South. For Hunter and Robinson, "the South" isn't *just* "shorthand for systematic inequality and racism"; it's also, as for Tisby, shorthand for African American culture: "Black migrants brought and bring 'The South'—Black regional customs, worldviews and cultures—with them to their new homes in destinations across urban America."[54] Sharing little in common with their other "South," even less with neo-

Confederate or *Southern Living* Souths—detached entirely from geographical region—this South was obviously a construction, one that seemed useful and meaningful to the group it assembled. With the South seemingly up for grabs, I argued in 2008 that there were simply many Souths, there for the taking.

In retrospect, this seems an overly optimistic view or at least an insufficiently pessimistic one, the result, in part, of my qualified acceptance of Francis Fukayama's end of history thesis. If liberal democracy had triumphed and countries housing McDonald's franchises never (or rarely) warred against one another, then the South seemed to be following the trend, its culture having largely succumbed to the superficialities and cosmetic attractions of what Stanley Fish calls "boutique multiculturalism." It seemed to generate softer tribalisms—the tribe of the 'mater sandwich, for example—compatible with liberal democracy, even if, at the fringes, it still produced a neo-Confederate or two, leading me to suggest "better a cyber-Confederacy than a real one."[55] That was a bad sentence to write in 2008, and the sentiment was wholly upended by Dylan Roof and Charleston. What I imagined, I think, was pretend Confederates quarantined in a chat room, a more or less harmless subculture whose views would remain absent from public discourse because if one spoke too proudly of the Confederacy in public, one risked being branded a racist. What I did not foresee was that the chat room would evolve into the public, that internet anonymity would catalyze explicit racist speech, and that the rise of social media would facilitate group assembly and antagonism in ways often said to be new and unexpected. We shouldn't—I shouldn't—have been surprised: the appearance of new media has often catalyzed new and powerful forms of group formation and conflict. For Benedict Anderson, the modern nation is inconceivable without the novel and the newspaper, while Niall Ferguson observes that the tumult of the seventeenth century derived in part, from the rise of print, which contributed a bit "to what ultimately became a Scientific Revolution" but devoted a great deal more attention to "alchemy, astrology, witch-finding and obscure arguments about the difference between transubstantiation and consubstantiation—in short, to superstition."[56] Without the cardboard box, an invention of the late nineteenth century, there's no Aunt Jemima. Given, as I've argued, that memes flourish in symbolic environments, is it any wonder that the harder-edged, more conspiratorial memes of Dixie have replicated there?[57]

Novel and Depleted Memes

My primary subject, however, is southern memes ostensibly detached from Dixie—novel memes like football or the tomato sandwich or depleted memes like southern hospitality or "sense of place" so far removed from their original scenes of disputation and group formation that they might be viewed as altogether benign. Where the latter are concerned, I am inclined to agree with Szczesiul, who argues that "considered from an ethical perspective, *there is no usable past* when it comes to the southern hospitality of slavery and segregation."[58] To the ethical argument might be added a functional one: if the hospitality meme has, so to speak, bad DNA, weaker genetic expressions of it often seem to say the same thing sotto voce. At *Southern Living*'s online platform, hospitality no longer relies on the crude stereotypes evident at Aunt Fanny's Cabin or the slightly updated variant in Hyatt's Charlie Ferguson, but in 2022, the magazine still wanted to bring back (and you will, too!) the southern hospitality of front porches and sweet tea—as captured in a piece accompanied by black and white photographs of fifty-six southerners, all white, taken between 1930 and 1970, suggesting a covert desire to . . . make the South great again.[59]

Similarly, the silencing of Aunt Jemima meant that she could no longer say, as she had in a 1921 ad recalling her debut at the 1893 World's Fair, things like, "Lawzee, we ain't nevah gwine be able to make enuf pancakes fo' all dem white folks."[60] But as Manring observes in connection with her silent and visually updated mutation—a properly undead Aunt Jemima—the "argument that the remade Aunt Jemima is significantly different from the old version seems incorrect, because we cannot separate the elements that make Aunt Jemima, regardless of whether she herself is made over."[61]

Leaving aside Aunt Jemima (as PepsiCo actually did in 2022), is it possible for southern memes to stop being Dixie memes—for southern hospitality, say, to "separate the elements" enough to divest itself of its plantation origin? Szczesiul, for example, considers Alabama's official state tourism website, which promises that the state will deliver "Southern hospitality" and explains that "a truly authentic Southern experience is about something far more memorable than a stately plantation or frosty mint julep. While you'll find plenty of those in Alabama, the moments that best define our state are far more personal." Those moments include "the firm handshakes, the warm smiles, the generations of stories behind each delicious dish and homemade craft." In Alabama, you'll get to meet, personally, "third-generation restaurant owners who are still using the recipes taught to them as children," while the "tips you'll learn from locals" beat anything you'll learn from the website.[62] But even transferred to warm smiles, storied cuisine, and locality, the new hospitality is mnemonically linked to what you probably *thought* was memorable: the stately plantation enchanting the handshake that might otherwise seem like "just any old American handshake." (And if you want the plantations and juleps, there are plenty of those, too.)

In this effort to remediate hospitality, we see what McGehee finds in the merchandise offered by *Bitter Southerner*: salable items that in yet another attempt at progressive remediation "still ultimately project a singular and exceptional U.S. South . . . rooted in the categories that [Patricia] Yaeger, [Jon] Smith, and many others in southern studies have tried to complicate over the past twenty years." Of the wares offered by *Garden & Gun*, *Bitter Southerner*, and a range of southern-themed T-shirt companies, McGehee concludes that they "ultimately reduce the diverse and troubled region to a number of stock images and phrases" that "reinforc[e] the region's insularity and boundedness" and continue to equate "southern-ness with whiteness and wealth."[63] Since whiteness and wealth is where the South began, it's perhaps not surprising that that's where it continues to replicate most successfully, even if, as I've argued, Dixie memes have often worked just as well in consolidating the South through whiteness and deprivation.

The problem with remediation, as the editors of *Remediating Region* observe, is that it begins not with a region but a prior mediation of it, thus basing the new and improved South on the old, unimproved one. This is apparent, I suggest, in even the most novel memes. Take the tomato sandwich. A piece from *Garden & Gun* is just one among dozens revealed by a Google search that affirms the tomato sandwich's identity as "southern": "for many Southerners, nothing is better on a hot afternoon than juicy slices of perfectly ripe tomato layered with Kraft mayonnaise and a pinch of salt and pepper between two slices of white bread." Of course the mayonnaise *isn't* Kraft, but Duke's, which somewhere along the line became *our* mayonnaise. A version of the no true southerner test appears to be in the vicinity, which further browsing confirms. Not only do many southerners eat tomatoes sandwiches, many southerners write about them as well. Indeed, the sandwich "has been written and rewritten to the point where we all know how the writer will eat the sandwich: in an elderly relative's kitchen, what it will taste like: tomato still warm from the bush, tangy, sweet, like childhood, and what it reminds her of: a time that no longer exists, the good days." As tropes (and compulsive citations of tropes) accumulate, we learn that the "South's long hot summers are to blame for our tomato sandwich love affair" and that, in a gesture of support for southern exceptionalism, "if we get really Southern-specific, our tomatoes are the only ones truly big enough to spread across a piece of white bread." We learn of the sandwich's southern origins, first appearing in a 1911 edition of the *Alexandria (Va.) Gazette.*[64] Clearly, then, the tomato sandwich has clearly evolved into a southern meme. T-shirts confirm the conclusion. In addition to *Bitter Southerner*'s "Mayo and Tomato," there's a "southern classic" variant, "Mater Sandwich—Tried and True," in which Duke's mayo is visible, from Lady Gryphon, "Butter of the South," foregrounding the Duke's but including the sandwich, from Simply Southern, "'Mater Sammich: Fresh from the Garden," upping the dialect, from Southern Fried Cotton, and, finally, "Southern as a Tomato Sandwich" from It's a Southern Thing.

But what does it mean to be "southern as a tomato sandwich"? Of what notional South is Duke's mayonnaise the butter? As always, the stock images and phrases come thick and fast: the good old days, cotton, the "mater" rendered in dialect, an elderly relative's (surely a grandmother's) kitchen, long hot summers. Of necessity, the tomato is "fresh from the garden" (at best a home garden, at worst a local one); it cannot have come from Mexico (the origin of most tomatoes eaten in the Southeast). Inevitably, the mayonnaise is Duke's, not Miracle Whip, which we all know isn't even a mayonnaise (although Miracle Whip probably outsells Duke's in the Southeast).[65] A bit more demystification. Two years before it appeared in the *Alexandria Gazette*—as part of the teetotaler's (not southerner's) diet—two tomato sandwich recipes appear in *The Up-to-Date Sandwich Book*, published in Chicago.[66] Two decades before that, a newspaper in River Falls, Wisconsin, provided an entirely utilitarian recipe for the tomato sandwich: "prepare bread and butter for sandwiches and lay the tomato slices between the slices of bread."[67] (Possibly, the sandwich occurs wherever there are tomatoes, bread, a lack of bacon, and the conception of a sandwich.) Of twenty southern chefs corralled by *Garden & Gun*, fifteen declared Duke's to be their "go-to brand," but in a blind taste test, only seven preferred Duke's.[68] In support of Alton Brown's claim that "southern identity doesn't exist without food," Cooper and Knotts provide data showing that 16 per-

"Southern as a Tomato Sandwich" T-shirt. It's a Southern Thing merchandise.

cent of southerners regularly consume "fried tomatoes," as opposed to 13 percent of nonsoutherners. The MoonPie gap is larger at 14 percent to 5 percent. Assuming that southeasterners consume tomato sandwiches at roughly the MoonPie rate, we might conclude that a group identity is being conjured from a statistical variation.

But group boundaries aren't drawn that way. They delineate, however tenuously, an absolute inside and outside. If southerners are three times more likely than Wisconsinites to eat tomato sandwiches, they are infinitely more likely to wear a T-shirt saying that tomato sandwiches are their thing, a *southern* thing, even if the sandwich was invented in Wisconsin and is the eighth (or eighteenth) most popular sandwich consumed in the Southeast. Actual tomato sandwich consumption, I suggest, is no more relevant to the assembly of southerners than actual Cavalier ancestry was in 1850. As the jukebox is to Reed's localism, so the T-shirt is to the tomato sandwich: a medium in which the notional South is reproduced by means of a meme.

True, the southerners—that is, customer bases—in question might differ from brand to brand. Southern Fried Cotton aims for the upscale good old boy who hunts, fishes, flies the American flag, and owns a dog: a "pinch of country and a dash of country club," as the website puts it.[69] It offers a "Southern Belle collection," but it's all dogs, cows, watermelons, and country churches. *Bitter Southerner*, of course, steers well clear of southern belles (since it doesn't allow hoop skirts), and its understated fonts signal "Dolly&/Tammy&/Wynonna&/Emmylou" and "Zora&/Alice&/Maya&/Jesmyn." Of the southerner's purported "hunger for tomatoes," it insists that "tomatoes have been part of Southern culture from the beginning" but is decent enough to worry that "our hunger for them means too many people in the fields don't get treated fairly."[70] But whether the southerner in question loves Trump or hates him, their assembly vis-à-vis the tomato sandwich presumes the existence of a South that remains, as Cable puts it, a "sort 'o something" as "portable and intangible as—as—the souls in our bodies."[71]

It may seem perverse to argue with T-shirts so apparently innocent, but I maintain that these T-shirts are still in an argument. Just as *Southern Living* reconstructs from a South made of Bull Connor and the KKK a South made of azaleas and football, so *Bitter Southerner* reconstructs its South in reaction to folks' perception of southerners who are too tied to tradition. The text of its "Bitter Southerner Be Shirt" makes this clear in its injunction to "be the smart Southerner among those who think there is no such thing."[72] This isn't advice for persons viewing the shirt, but a signal that the person wearing it is the kind who might be thought imaginary. In gesturing to a South of exceptional tomatoes, home gardens, and long, hot summers, the tomato sandwich, I suspect, is saying something similar. Recall that Wisconsinites, who have better claim to the sandwich, have never defended, or been asked to defend, residential segregation in Milwaukee or the events of Kenosha as part of a way of life. To be as "southern as a tomato sandwich" declares one's innocence of being "southern as a hoop skirt-admiring oaf" but accepts the charge of belonging to a culture to which tomatoes have been important "from the beginning." Tomato sandwiches, then, do what "sense of place" does for Wilson and R&B does for Lady A: they retcon a culture that "has been there all along" but that bears little relation to historical group formation (since no Confederate soldier or Dixiecrat defended a "culture" defined by tomatoes) and is even less connected with the stigmata of the present, accusations involving sandwich consumption being largely unknown.

The tomato sandwich, then, fills a need to both construct and protect a South projected backward in time—a South not unencumbered with historical baggage but nevertheless not defined by it. But in thus inoculating the South, such efforts typically replicate the stock images and phrases originally used to render the baggage organic.[73] If, as I've argued, the South's foundation wasn't, as Alexander Stephens argued, slavery but the magic that turned slavery into a plantation and if the cardinal test of a southerner wasn't, as Phillips argued, white supremacy but the enchantments that transformed an unprecedented system of racial discrimination into an organic way of life, it would appear reasonable to assume that the memes of Dixie are pretty good at that sort of thing. Defending peculiarity or recovering it as distinction seems the primary function of Dixie memes, which perhaps should be regarded skeptically for that reason alone.

As I've mentioned, this represents a departure from my previous view, a shift partially occasioned by Eric Gary Anderson, Taylor Hagood, and Daniel Cross Turner, who argue in their introduction to *Undead Souths* that "the ephemeral reproductions of clichéd Southernness" I take up in *The Real South* could be seen as "aiding and abetting a kind of cultural zombieism," constituting a "submission to empty repetition of past cultural modes, a will-less recitation of past 'citations' of what signifies southernism."[74] This put a negative spin on what I had seen as a mostly benign trajectory, but it also introduced an idea of will-lessness that I had not considered. In understanding the "materials" of southernism as subject to improvisation and play, I had followed the example of O'Brien, who, in developing the idea of the South as an idea, typically reverts to a language of volition. The South, for O'Brien, is "especially reliant for its survival upon an act of emotional and intellectual will"; it "has always been an effort of will," although there may be "evidence that the will is lacking." If, as he claims in 2007, "Southerners are people who can find a way to say, 'The South is . . .' or 'Southerners are . . . ,'" is the South "something still worth inventing?"[75]

In retrospect, the zombie analogy, with its emphasis on "will-less recitation," seems a more accurate way of describing what I had called "cultural reproduction." I am continually struck by the capacity of memes to conjure a South we think we know and therefore *do know* (because we know it) and to do so in a way that resists any effort to *deconstruct* or dismantle them.[76] I mentioned earlier my failed stint as an art critic, during which, I'm certain, I persuaded no one that a distinctive "sense of place" wasn't really a southern thing. Perry's acute observations will do little to dislodge the southern signifiers listed on the back cover of her book. Latour observes that when speakers invoke the "big picture," they often make a hand gesture outlining a shape no bigger than a pumpkin.[77] As far as I'm concerned, that's a useful idea to keep in mind when holding a tomato sandwich, but I harbor no illusions that "southern as a tomato sandwich" will cease to summon the "big picture" of a notional South.[78] When I hear, as I did recently, three—possibly four—Dixie memes in a radio ad for flood insurance, I am tempted to accept Dawkins's claim that memes are mind viruses, that "a cultural trait may have evolved in the way that it has, simply because it is *advantageous to itself*."[79]

As I've argued, memes are not exactly "cultural traits," but their ability to ensure the "resilience of southern identity" is fully and interestingly evident in Cooper and Knotts's book, which goes to great lengths to defend the notional South. I've noted that the authors have "no doubt" that "Black southerners have . . . always considered themselves southerners," despite also having no evidence that they did. Their desire for an always inclusive southern identity leads them to conclude that Reed's conception of southern ethnicity is "unnecessarily exclusionary" and "diminishes the power of the concept of regional identity as a true uniting force." Southern identity does, however, have a "dark side" that dates back, apparently, to the era of Strom Thurmond and George Wallace. But in a classic gesture of inoculation, the use of southern identity to "advance a populist and often racist political agenda" is declared a "misuse" that "has allowed white supremacist attitudes to be conflated with other forms of southern identity in many people's minds." Lest anyone doubt that the authors use the proper form, they assure the reader that "you won't find any supersized belt buckles in our closets, jacked up trucks in our driveways, or Confederate flags on our properties." Southern distinctiveness, or the perception thereof, seems self-evident. There is a "stronger case" to be made for the latter, but it is often relegated to parentheses. There is, for example, "good evidence that distinctiveness (or at least perceived distinctiveness) is a precursor to identity," since "were the South not a distinct place (at least in people's minds)," would *Garden & Gun* have such a subscription base? Would Mississippi taxpayers support the Center for the Study of Southern Culture at the University of Mississippi?[80]

When we get around to the nature of the distinctiveness, we find that it is actually *distinction*. "One of the clearest indications of southern culture," they write, "relates to the 'southern way of life,'" which is "marked by hospitality, manners, and a slower pace of life." The culture, then, is confirmed by this way of life, which is confirmed by focus group members who reliably produce the talking points (using "strikingly similar language") and just as reliably assert that "northerners do not hold or appreciate the same values": "The South has often been referred to as a 'negative reference point' for the nation, but we saw considerable evidence that the non-South, particularly the northeastern states, provided a negative reference point for the self-identified southerners in the focus groups." *But*? When have southerners *ever* accepted their status as "negative reference point" and not turned the memic tables on their Yankee accusers? When has a group identity ever functioned on the basis of precise and accurate self-description? That they believe that one of "more surprising discoveries from talking with southerners was how much of their southern identity is defined in contrast to people from other regions" is itself surprising, since that that's how identity generally works. Southerners have been "frustrated and embarrassed" with how they are "portrayed in the media" ever since John C. Calhoun complained of the "incendiary spirit" spreading through the northern pulpit and press.[81] It's been over a century since Walter Hines Page complained that foremost among the "combination of forces that we mean when we speak of 'The South'" was the defensive "self-conscious 'Southerner' . . . thrust upon [us]," a dead "shadow 'Southerner' . . . which every living man of us has to carry."[82]

Without knowing it, Cooper and Knotts have identified the ur-narrative of southern identity: in response to the (real or imagined) slander of Yankees, southerners say and think good things about themselves, which are then assigned to a South from which, it is believed, they have emerged organically. Southerners are not only fed up with northern media representations of themselves but with northerners too. Several focus group members relate frustrating experiences with, as one Black participant puts it, "people up North [who] have a perception about how we are down South." But in "highlighting just how sensitive southerners are to how they are perceived," Cooper and Knotts do not consider the possibility that being seen as "dum[b] hick[s]" might explain why several participants cite "the land itself as being important to their southern identity." Although all participants are "residents of a medium-sized, somewhat densely populated city," many testify to "an appreciation of rural life," including Jack, a Black participant for whom walking barefoot, "a country boy type of thing," distinguishes him from northerners "who are not as rugged." Of "hospitality, manners, and pace of life," Cooper and Knotts are struck by "the consistency of the comments" and their apparent "simplistic or stereotypes view of the South" but are compelled to accept them as the "mores and folkways . . . at the top of southerners' minds." For William Graham Sumner, the top of the mind was exactly where mores and folkways couldn't be, but the error effectively captures the capacity of memes to constitute the self-evidence of a South rendered self-evident. Unsurprisingly, the coherence of that South breaks down upon the introduction of race relations, the Civil War, and the Confederate flag, which reveal "parts of southern identity [that] drive wedges between white and black southerners."[83]

O'Brien argues that given its dependence on a "willingness to believe in and assert a mutuality," the South would fracture or "diminish in emotional energy" under the centrifugal forces of multiculturalism.[84] For the participants in the focus group, this appears untrue in several ways. First, the South "at the top of the mind" seems to be there without effort but is nevertheless full of emotional energy. Moreover, citations of the South conspicuously fail to affirm a mutuality. Although Black participants effortlessly call to mind a South responding to northern stigmata, they are just as quick to cite the white South—sometimes just "the South"—as antagonist. Keith is "proud to be a southerner, because I separate being a black southerner from being a white southerner," later indicating relief that, at least, "black people in the South feel safe again," since "the southern people . . . don't go around snatching people out of their homes and killing them." Claire remarks that "[white] southerners lost the war but they can still win by wearing the [Confederate] flag," the parenthetical "white" having been provided by the authors. The tensions here are unsurprising; many "black Souths" are racially exclusive, including Hunter and Robinson's, "the South" for them serving as "shorthand" for both "systematic inequality and racism" *and* "Black regional customs, worldviews and cultures" transported from the Southeast to rest of the nation. For their part, white participants similarly fail to assert a mutuality. Several report "tension" and distrust between races in the South, while Keith notes that "it will take twenty years for me not to think white guy or blond white girl when you say southerner." Pam, a white teacher, reports advising a Black student that he "should not be bringing up slavery," since, as she tells him, "you are not the only culture, or ethnic background, that has been oppressed."[85]

That the South fails to assemble a community—even an imagined community—that accommodates all southeasterners is perhaps as unsurprising as the failure of monotheism to produce a single body of believers. And yet one is struck by the capacity of "southern culture" and "the southern way of life" to conjure precisely that idea: a singular "southern identity" that, minus a wedge issue here or there, derives from and confirms a common set of mores and folkways. From their inception, the memes of Dixie have created the impression that the South grew southerners—a *kind* of person—and accommodated all persons living in the region, whether they were southerners or not. But evolving in defense of a southern *us* against "those people over there," they have never realized the impression and have usually done quite the opposite. By any historical math, what Cooper and Knotts characterize as "the dark side" of southern identity has constituted most of it, which raises the question of whether the South, rather than being remediated, should instead be considered irremediable. To the extent that the South continues to have *lost* the Civil War and to have been the *victim* of Reconstruction, I fully agree with Smith that we should simply shoot the jukebox—or, to alter the analogy, drive a stake through the heart of the zombie memes.[86] Of course, that's both easy for me to say (since, having little stake in the South, I have little to protect) and somewhat beside the point (since I have no idea what the stake would consist of). By any identitarian calculus, we have ample evidence regarding the South of what Manring claims of one its signature memes. The image of the mammy, he writes, had a "utility . . . in white minds, black minds, male minds, female minds. She was above all, and continues to be, a useful person."[87] Just so for the South, which has long been effective in persuading minds that they belong to a kind of person—surely a predictor of fecundity in an age in which identity serves as the coin of the realm. The South has never lacked a receptive audience and doesn't lack one today on any of the jukeboxes (there's more than one) playing its song. One jukebox plays hospitality, slower pace of life, Lynyrd Skynyrd, "Rich Men North of Richmond," the Confederate flag, hoop skirts, and "heritage, not hate." Another plays hospitality, slower pace of life, "all y'all," a carefully curated mix of R&B and country, tomato sandwiches, and "be the smart Southerner among those who think there is no such thing." North of the Mason-Dixon, a third plays "there is no such thing as a smart southerner," the ballad of Bull Connor, Neil Young's "Southern Man," and other songs of innocence. The Black jukebox is the most complicated and tactical, at times citing Haley on "our southern ancestors, black and white" but more often borrowing from Haley's *Roots* and from jukeboxes 2 and 3, usually without asserting a "southern identity," "way of life," or "communality of interest" shared with everyone inhabiting the region.

It would be better, in my opinion, to *think less* of the South or at least to recognize that what Greeson calls the "South that we hold collectively in our minds" (1) isn't a "real place," (2) isn't always held collectively, and (3) often depends on a very few stock images, phrases, or signifiers that notionally integrate a "big picture" of eleven to seventeen states (or parts of them) comprising more than a third of the U.S. population. But although its memes may appear timeless, inevitable, and "beyond dispute" (it's important that they do if they are to function), many of them emerged amid disputation and historical contingency, often in defense of slavery and then segregation, serving to express, as "difference," an antagonism between North and South that maps badly on both the regions so designated and the persons who inhabit them. Is the southerner a racist? A lover of tomato sandwiches? A person distinctively affected by a warm climate? By the Battle of Gettysburg? To ask the questions is to realize that they have no answers.

Alternatively, we might *think more* about the South as a way of considering whether our ideas about it are actually beliefs. If so, are the beliefs good ideas? What groups do they assemble? What functions do they serve? If, as even many neo-Confederates would concede, the South was a bad idea both in 1850 and a century later, when, precisely, did it become a good idea? If, more pointedly and specifically, the South evolved in an ethnonationalist defense of a slaveholding people and, in its current form, generates the perception of temporal continuity with that group, how much inoculation against its "the dark side" is enough? Why not instead inoculate against the memes that naturalize the South as self-evident and inevitable?

As I've said, these are easy questions for me to ask and answer, since, haunted little by Page's "shadow Southerner," I feel little compulsion to defend, or even define, the South. For persons who see and feel themselves to be southerners or who see others that way, the questions will be harder but perhaps useful to consider.

Notes

Introduction. A South Made of Memes

1. John Shelton Reed, *Minding the South* (Columbia: University of Missouri Press, 2003), 109.

2. Eudora Welty, "Place in Fiction," in *The Eye of the Story: Selected Essays and Reviews* (New York: Vintage, 1979), 132. My recollection of Welty's "Place in Fiction" at the time of the conference was, of course, less precise, although I did remember (and convey) that Welty says nothing about a distinctively southern sense of place.

3. "Southern United States Literature," Wikipedia, https://en.wikipedia.org/wiki/Southern_United_States_literature.

4. William Gilmore Simms, "Americanism in Literature," in *Views and Reviews in American Literature, History, and Fiction* (New York: Wiley and Putnam, 1845), 6.

5. A. B. Meek, *Songs and Poems of the South* (Mobile, Ala.: S. H. Goetzel, 1857), v. "Racy of the soil" was a term borrowed from the *Nation*, a nineteenth-century Irish newspaper associated with the Young Ireland nationalist movement; the term featured prominently in the writings of the Young America literary movement.

6. Quoted in C. Hugh Holman, *The Roots of Southern Writing* (Athens: University of Georgia Press, 1972), 78. In *The Impending Crisis in the South* (1858; repr., New York: A. B. Burdick, 1860), Hinton Rowan Helper argues that the South had no literature, reporting that "this was virtually admitted by more than one speaker at the late 'Southern Convention' at Savannah. Said a South Carolina orator on that occasion: 'It is important that the South should have a literature of her own, to defend her principles and her rights;' a sufficiently plain concession that she has not, now, such a literature" (386).

7. "American Literature—Northern and Southern," *De Bow's Review* 24, no. 4 (1858): 176

8. J. B. Wardlaw, *Southern Literature: Its Status and Outlook* (Macon, Ga.: J. W. Burke, 1890), 9, 18, 21. In *Life on the Mississippi*, Mark Twain argues that Scott had similarly catalyzed southern nationalism and feeling, with disastrous consequences.

9. Allen Tate, "The Profession of Letters in the South," in *Allen Tate: Essays of Four Decades* (Chicago: Swallow Press, 1968), 517–34; Lewis P. Simpson, *The Dispossessed Garden* (Athens: University of Georgia Press, 1975), 38.

10. Louis D. Rubin, *Writers of the Modern South: The Faraway Country* (Seattle: University of Washington Press, 1963), 19.

11. Donald Davidson, *The Attack on Leviathan: Regionalism and Nationalism in the United States* (1938; repr., Abington, UK: Routledge, 2017), 96; "The Artist as Southerner," *Saturday Review*, May 15, 1926, 782.

12. Frederick J. Hoffman, "The Sense of Place," in *South: Modern Southern Literature in Its Cultural Setting*, ed. Louis D. Rubin Jr. and Robert D. Jacobs (Garden City, N.Y: Doubleday, 1961), 60–75, 63, 64, 68, 70.

13. Ian Hacking, *The Social Construction of What?* (Cambridge, Mass.: Harvard University Press, 1999), 6, 12.

14. Jon Smith, "Toward a Post-Postpolitical Southern Studies: On the Limits of the 'Creating and Consuming' Paradigm," in *Creating and Consuming the American South*, ed. Martyn Bone, Brian E. Ward, and William A. Link (Gainesville: University Press of Florida, 2015), 83.

15. Michael Kreyling, "A Southern Dissensus?," *Southern Literary Journal* 19, no. 2 (1987): 103.

16. Hacking, *The Social Construction of What?*, 6.

17. Patricia Yaeger, *Dirt and Desire: Reconstructing Southern Women's Writing, 1930–1990* (Chicago: University of Chicago Press, 2000), 34.

18. Jennifer Rae Greeson, "What Was 'Southern Literature'?," *American Literary History* 32, no. 3 (2020): 575. The trend away from the pseudonationalist model of literary history is evident in my and Greeson's coedited *Keywords for Southern Studies* (Athens: University of Georgia Press, 2016), which was originally conceived as a successor to Rubin's *History of Southern Literature*, and in Harilous Stecopoulos's edited volume *History of the Literature of the U.S. South* (Cambridge: Cambridge University Press, 2021), which explicitly rejects the Tainean model of literary history.

19. Leigh Anne Duck, "Southern Nonidentity," *Safundi: The Journal of South African and American Studies* 9, no. 3 (2008): 329.

20. Scott Romine, "Where is Southern Literature?: The Practice of Place in a Postsouthern Age," in *South to a New Place*, ed. Suzanne W. Jones and Sharon Monteith (Baton Rouge: Louisiana State University Press, 2002), 40.

21. Larry J. Griffin and Ashley B. Thompson, "Enough about the Disappearing South: What about the Disappearing Southerner?," *Southern Cultures* 9, no. 3 (2003): 51–52; Christopher A. Cooper and H. Gibbs Knotts, *The Resilience of Southern Identity* (Chapel Hill: University of North Carolina Press, 2017).

22. Jennifer Rae Greeson, *Our South: Geographic Fantasy and the Rise of National Literature* (Cambridge, Mass.: Harvard University Press, 2010), 1.

23. See Bruno Latour, *Reassembling the Social: An Introduction to Actor-Network Theory* (Oxford: Oxford University Press, 2005), 29.

24. "How do people in the American South deal with the extreme heat and humidity in the summer?," Quora question, https://www.quora.com/How-do-people-in-the-American-South-deal-with-the-extreme-heat-and-humidity-in-the-summer, accessed May 23, 2020.

25. Richard Dawkins, *The Extended Selfish Gene* (Oxford: Oxford University Press, 1989), 254, 253, 249.

26. Dawkins, *The Extended Selfish Gene*, 257, 259.

27. Dawkins, *The Extended Selfish Gene*, 423, 424. Reconsidering his example of Darwin as a meme, Dawkins suggests that scientific ideas differ from other memes because "their rightness and wrongness can be tested" (426).

28. See Jonathan Haidt, *The Righteous Mind: Why Good People are Divided by Politics and Religion* (New York: Vintage, 2013), 288–92.

29. Josephine Humphreys, *Rich in Love* (1987; repr., New York: Penguin, 1992), 31. More precisely, the idea that the South is subject to "extreme heat and humidity" (like Darwin's theory) *may* be true, but it only becomes a meme when it replicates to define a group boundary.

30. Humphreys, *Rich in Love*, 31.

31. The assertion that memes help create groups that will then

replicate the meme is similar to the argument offered by Robert A. Paul in *Moses and Civilization: The Meaning behind Freud's Myth* (New Haven, Conn.: Yale University Press, 1996), which I came across late in this project. Paul argues that "a 'memic' or cultural replicator accomplishes its work by channeling the motivations and capacities of human actors into activities that result in the reproduction of copies of the meme." According to Paul, the meme "produces a population of humans who are 'like' it, in the sense that they actualize its instructions" (186). As I make clear, I am more skeptical of the "instructional" capacity of memes.

32. Dawkins, *The Extended Selfish Gene*, 255.

33. M. M. Manring, *Slave in a Box: The Strange Career of Aunt Jemima* (Charlottesville: University Press of Virginia, 1998), 7.

34. To state the obvious, memes often have different histories than the history they reference. As Wesley Moody has shown in *Demon of the Lost Cause* (Columbia: University of Missouri Press, 2011), Sherman as the "demon of the Lost Cause" dates to the 1880s. Sherman, then, was not yet "Sherman" in 1874, although he had burned Atlanta a decade earlier (105–10).

35. Even if Faulkner can't be said to belong to southerners per se, at the very least he can be said to belong to *their culture*. Walter Benn Michaels considers a similar question of how aspects of a culture can claimed by members of a group who may not have knowledge or direct experience of them in *The Trouble with Diversity: How We Learned to Love Identity and Ignore Inequality* (New York: Holt, 2006), 43–45.

36. Ed Tarkington, "The Troubled Task of Defining Southern Literature in 2021," *Literary Hub*, January 22, 2021, https://lithub.com/the-troubled-task-of-defining-southern-literature-in-2021/.

37. Heather Cox Richardson, *How the South Won the Civil War: Oligarchy, Democracy, and the Continuing Fight for the Soul of America* (New York: Oxford University Press, 2020); Albion Tourgée, "The Apotheosis of the Kuklux Klan," *The Continent: An Illustrated Weekly Magazine* 6, no. 129 (1884): 153; Edward A. Pollard, *The Lost Cause Regained* (New York: G. W. Carleton, 1868), 13.

38. Adolph L. Reed Jr., *The South: Jim Crow and Its Afterlives* (London: Verso, 2022), 86. As Reed observes, such folk knowledge "can be impervious to contradiction by study and experience" (86).

39. Immanuel Wallerstein, "What Can One Mean by Southern Culture?," in *The Evolution of Southern Culture,* ed. Numan V. Bartley (Athens: University of Georgia Press, 1988), 8.

40. Donald M. Nonini, "Critique: Creating the Transnational South," in *The American South in a Global World,* ed. James L. Peacock, Harry L. Watson, and Carrie R. Matthews (Chapel Hill: University of North Carolina Press, 2005), 254–55.

41. Antony Flew, *Thinking about Thinking: Or, Do I Sincerely Want to Be Right?* (Glasgow: Fontana, 1975), 47.

42. George Washington Cable, *John March, Southerner* (New York: Charles Scribner's Sons, 1894), 326, 327.

43. John Shelton Reed, *The Enduring South: Subcultural Persistence in Mass Society* (1972; repr., Chapel Hill: University of North Carolina Press, 1986), 9. Reed adds that "differences in culture and demography" in a given region constitute "no-less-important 'climates'" than climate, soil, and terrain (9). I suggest that the "intrinsic" aspects of religion and southernness are more similar than Reed suggests. Just as a child born into a Christian family or community is likely to adopt certain beliefs about Christ, so a child born into the southern equivalent is more likely to adopt certain beliefs about the South, and to become, by analogy, a southian. The climate and soil, I suspect, have little to do with it.

44. C. Hugh Holman, *Three Modes of Southern Fiction: Ellen Glasgow, William Faulkner, Thomas Wolfe* (1966; repr., Athens: University of Georgia Press, 2008), 1–2, 2, 4, xiii, 7. That climate, terrain, demography, and "culture" (in any preidentitarian sense) vary widely within the region (and even neighborhood) is a truism, and so arguments such as Holman's that there are many Souths are not eye opening. Why they remain "Souths" in the absence of a shared climate, terrain, etc. is a more difficult question.

45. Louis D. Rubin Jr., introduction, to *The History of Southern Literature,* ed. Rubin, Blyden Jackson, Rayburn S. Moore, Lewis P. Simpson, and Thomas Daniel Young (Baton Rouge: Louisiana State University Press, 1985), 5.

46. V. S. Naipaul, *A Turn in the South* (New York: Vintage, 1990), 105, emphasis added.

47. Latour, *Reassembling the Social,* 33.

48. Edward B. Tylor, *Primitive Cultures,* vol. 1 (London: John Murray, 1871), 1; T. S. Eliot, *Notes toward the Definition of Culture* (London: Faber and Faber, 1948), 31; Arjun Appadurai, *Mo-*

dernity at Large: Cultural Dimensions of Globalization (Minneapolis: University of Minnesota Press, 1996), 14, 15; Stuart Hall, "Who Needs Identity?," in *Questions of Cultural Identity*, ed. Stuart Hall and Paul du Gay (London: Sage Publications, 1996), 3–4.

49. Bruno Latour, *Science in Action: How to Follow Scientists and Engineers through Society* (Cambridge, Mass.: Harvard University Press, 1987), 201.

50. Janet E. Halley, "'Like Race' Arguments," in *What's Left of Theory: New Work on the Politics of Literary Theory*, ed. Judith Butler, John Guillory, and Kendall Thomas (New York: Routledge, 2000), 41.

51. Fredric Jameson, "On Cultural Studies," in *The Identity in Question*, ed. John Rajchman (London: Routledge, 1995), 271. Latour similarly emphasizes the importance to group formation of an "anti-group . . . designated as being empty, archaic, dangerous, obsolete, and so on" (*Reassembling the Social*, 32).

52. James C. Cobb, *Away down South: A History of Southern Identity* (New York: Oxford University Press, 2005), 2.

53. Waldo W. Braden, *The Oral Tradition in the South* (Baton Rouge: Louisiana State University Press, 1983), 4.

54. Robert Penn Warren, *The Legacy of the Civil War* (1961; repr., Lincoln: University of Nebraska Press, 1998), 54. For the record, my analogous moment of epiphany regarding the South's dependence on "the North" came during the 2018 SSSL conference, when Jay Watson suggested that a revised edition of *Keywords for Southern Studies* should include the keyword "North."

55. W. J. Cash, *The Mind of the South* (1941; repr., New York: Vintage, 1969), 68.

56. Cash, *The Mind of the South*, x.

57. Michael O'Brien, *The Idea of the American South, 1920–1941* (Baltimore, Md.: Johns Hopkins University Press, 1979), 214. For Cash, O'Brien says, "perception was not a footnote to positivist reality, but reality a footnote to perception" (215).

58. Latour, *Reassembling the Social*, 24.

59. Brad Casey, "Why Are Dumb Canadians Waving the Confederate Flag?" *Vice*, March 7, 2013, https://www.vice.com/en/article/5gqw7n/why-are-dumb-canadians-waving-the-confederate-flag.

Chapter 1. The South under Construction

1. John C. Calhoun, "Speech on the Reception of Abolition Petitions," in *Speeches of John C. Calhoun*, vol. 2 (New York: Appleton, 1853), 630, 632, 631.

2. Larry E. Tise, "The 'Positive Good' Thesis and Proslavery Arguments in Britain and America," in *Proslavery: A History of the Defense of Slavery in America, 1701–1840* (Athens: University of Georgia Press, 1987), 97.

3. Rives quoted in *Register of Debates in Congress, 24th Congress, 2nd Session* (Washington, D.C.: Gales and Seaton, 1837), 722, 721.

4. Calhoun, "Speech on the Reception of Abolition Petitions," 630, 627.

5. Allen Tate, "A Southern Mode of the Imagination," in *Allen Tate: Essays of Four Decades* (Chicago: Swallow Press, 1968), 589.

6. Walter Benn Michaels, *The Shape of the Signifier: 1967 to the End of History* (Princeton, N.J.: Princeton University Press, 2006), 30.

7. Rives quoted in *Register of Debates in Congress, 24th Congress, 2nd Session*, 722, 721.

8. Calhoun, "Speech on the Reception of Abolition Petitions," 630, emphasis added.

9. Tate, "A Southern Mode of the Imagination," 589.

10. Allen Tate, "Narcissus as Narcissus," in *Allen Tate*, 597.

11. Tate, "A Southern Mode of the Imagination," 588, 587.

12. Roland Barthes, "Myth Today," in *A Barthes Reader*, ed. Susan Sontag (New York: Hill and Wang, 1982), 101, 102, 101–2, 105, 105.

13. Tate, "A Southern Mode of the Imagination," 587.

14. John Shelton Reed, *One South: An Ethnic Approach to Regional Culture* (Baton Rouge: Louisiana State University Press, 1982), 4–5. I once heard a well-known southern historian argue similarly that "if we're not talking about the South, we're just talking." My response is that there is no South until people start talking about it.

15. It might be noted that the History Channel started out with something like history and ended up with nearly two hundred episodes of *Ancient Aliens*.

16. Gladstone quoted in Howard Jones, *Crucible of Power: A History of American Foreign Relations to 1913* (Wilmington, Del.: Scholarly Resources, 2002), 211.

17. Walter Hines Page, *The Southerner* (1909; repr., Columbia: University of South Carolina Press, 2008), 150, 46.

18. Samuel Phillips Day, *Down South; or, An Englishman's Experience at the Seat of the American War*, vol. 1 (London: Hurst and Blackett, 1862), 193, 172, 150, 175, 175.

19. Hugh Blair Grigsby, *The Virginia Convention of 1776* (Richmond, Va.: J. W. Randolph, 1855), 38, 6, 5, 38, 37.

20. W. J. Cash, *The Mind of the South* (1941; repr., New York: Vintage, 1969), 4.

21. Daniel Joseph Singal, *The War Within: From Victorian to Modernist Thought in the South, 1919–1945* (Chapel Hill: University of North Carolina Press, 1982), 11.

22. Charles Wells Russell, *Roebuck: A Novel* (New York: M. Doolady, 1866), 208.

23. David Hackett Fisher, *Albion's Seed: Four British Folkways in America* (New York: Oxford University Press, 1989), 300, 304. On the question of Virginia's early myth making as a domain of yeomen and/or aristocrats, see Richard Gray, *Writing the South: Ideas of an American Region* (1986; repr., Baton Rouge: Louisiana State University Press, 1997), 1–24. Gray observes that the "planters of the Old Dominion never managed, even in their own judgement, to create an indigenous aristocratic culture" and argues that the proto-southern celebration of the yeoman farmer in the work of Jefferson and John Taylor of Caroline "unwillingly assum[ed] a position later to be held by the South as a whole: that of a conscious and declining minority within a young and growing nation" (17, 23).

24. Mark Twain, *Life on the Mississippi* (Boston: James R. Osgood, 1883), 467, 468, 469.

25. See Elizabeth Fox-Genovese and Eugene Genovese, *The Mind of the Master Class* (Cambridge: Cambridge University Press, 2005), 329–64.

26. "Tournament," *Richmond (Va.) Daily Dispatch*, September 21, 1854, 3.

27. D. R. Hundley, *Social Relations in Our Southern States* (New York: Henry B. Price, 1860), 175.

28. Kwame Anthony Appiah, *The Lies That Bind: Rethinking Identity* (New York: Liveright, 2018), 20–23.

29. John Pendleton Kennedy, *Swallow Barn; or, A Sojourn in the Old Dominion*, vol. 1 (Philadelphia: Carey and Lea, 1832), 53, 54.

30. Michael O'Brien, *Conjectures of Order: Intellectual Life in the American South, 1810–1860*, vol. 1 (Chapel Hill: University of North Carolina Press, 2004), 309–15, 315; William Alexander Caruthers, *The Cavaliers of Virginia; or, The Recluse of Jamestown* (New York: Harper and Brothers, 1834), 4.

31. "Speech of Mr. Wise," *Hillsborough (N.C.) Recorder*, April 4, 1839, 1.

32. Abel Parker Upshur, "The Partisan Leader (A Review of Tucker's novel)," *Southern Literary Messenger* 3, no. 1 (1837): 80. Interestingly, Tucker's novel takes places during an American civil war set to occur in 1849, twelve years after its date of publication. As "political speculation," Upshur concludes in his review, the novel was "probably too correct" (80).

33. Calvin H. Wiley, *The North Carolina Reader* (Philadelphia: Lippincott, Grambo, 1851), 132, 9, 89.

34. W. H. Trescot, "South Carolina: A Colony and a State," *De Bow's Review* 2, n.s., no. 6 (1859): 672, 673.

35. William R. Taylor, *Cavalier and Yankee: The Old South and American National Character* (1961; repr., New York: Oxford University Press, 1993), 15.

36. With evangelical fervor, *De Bow's* preached that "Commerce is King," the magazine's motto throughout the 1850s, hoping to stimulate "agricultural, commercial, and industrial progress" throughout the South .

37. New York, for example, depended heavily on southern trade. For an excellent account of this relationship, see Ritchey Devon Watson, *Grand Emporium/Mercantile Monster: The Antebellum South's Love-Hate Affair with New York City* (Baton Rouge: Louisiana State University Press, 2023).

38. Trescot, "South Carolina," 668, 672.

39. Joseph Glover Baldwin, *Flush Times of Alabama and Mississippi: A Series of Sketches* (1853; repr., New York: Appleton, 1858): 74–75.

40. The title of *De Bow's* changed regularly. At its 1846 inception, it was the *Commercial Review*. In 1850, it became the *Commercial Review of the South and West*, and the following year, *De Bow's Southern and Western Review*. By 1853, it had become *De*

Bow's Review: A Monthly Journal of Commerce, Agricultural, Manufacturers, Internal Improvements, Statistics, etc., etc., with variations in the subtitle emerging regularly thereafter.

41. An imprecise but telling metric is that during the 1830s the word "Cavalier" appears along with the words "Puritan," "Roundhead," or "Yankee" in thirteen newspaper articles available at the Library of Congress's Chronicling America website, none of them published before 1838. For the 1840s, the number is 48; for the 1850s, 139; for the 1860s, 280.

42. "This Is a War of Races," *Daily Richmond (Va.) Whig*, January 30, 1862, 1.

43. Trescot, "South Carolina," 668.

44. L. Johnson, *An Elementary Arithmetic Designed for Beginners* (Raleigh, N.C.: Branson and Farrar, 1864), 44; "Address of Gen. John B. Hood before the State Survivor's Association," *Columbia (S.C.) Daily Phoenix*, December 15, 1872, 3. The meme has dozens of variants, some of them hostile. The *Liberator*, for example, took pleasure at the war's close in recalling that but four years before, "Yankees were declared a cowardly set of abject creatures, a hundred of whom were scarcely a match for one of the chivalry"; see "Then and Now," *Liberator*, March 17, 1865, 1.

45. Edgar T. Thompson, "The South in Old and New Contexts," in *The South in Continuity and Change*, ed. John C. McKinney and Thompson (Durham, N.C.: Duke University Press, 1965), 458.

46. John C. Calhoun, "Report on the President's Message," in *Speeches of John C. Calhoun*, 195. The phrase "slaveholding South" was thus redundant, since the South was ipso facto connected with slaveholding.

47. Thomas Jefferson to John Holmes, in *The Portable Thomas Jefferson*, ed. Merrill D. Peterson (New York: Penguin, 1975), 568.

48. Calhoun, "Speech on the Reception of Abolition Petitions," 628, 629.

49. Henry Cleveland, *Alexander H. Stephens, in Public and Private, with Letters and Speeches, before, during, and since the War* (Philadelphia: National Publishing Company, 1866), 721.

50. William Henry Trescot, *The Position and Course of the South* (Charleston: Steam Power Press of Walker and James, 1850), n.p.

51. Hippolyte A. Taine, *History of English Literature*, vol. 1, trans. Henri Van Laun (New York: Holt and Williams, 1871), 11.

52. "Chivalry *alias* Calhounism," *Columbus (Miss.) Whig*, March 7, 1844, 1.

53. John George Metcalf, "Physiology of the Skin," in *Lectures Delivered before the American Institute of Instruction* (Boston: Marsh, Capen, Lyon and Webb, 1840), 46.

54. A. B. Meek, "Girl of the Sunny South," *Magnolia* 2, no. 1 (1843): 297; *The Sunny South: Or, the Southerner at Home*, ed. J. H. Ingraham (Philadelphia: G. G. Evans, 1860), 4.

55. Elizur Wright Jr., "The Sunny South," in *The North Star: The Poetry of Freedom, by Her Friends* (Philadelphia: Merrihew and Thompson, 1840), 12–13.

56. [Ralph Waldo Emerson], "American Civilization," *Atlantic Monthly* 9, no. 54 (1862): 504, 506.

57. George Fitzhugh, "Life and Liberty in America," *De Bow's Review* 2, n.s., no. 5 (1859): 521, 522.

58. Thomas Jefferson, *Notes on the State of Virginia* (Boston: Lilly and Wait, 1832), 170, 145, 170.

59. "Mr. Rowan's Address on Mr. Foot's Resolution, Monday, February 8, 1830." *Register of Debates in Congress: First Session of the Twenty-First Congress*, vol. 6 (Washington, D.C.: Gales and Seaton, 1830), 130–31.

60. Samuel A. Cartwright, "How to Save the Republic, and the Position of the South in the Union," *De Bow's Southern and Western Review* 1, n.s., no. 2 (1851): 195.

61. Cartwright, "How to Save the Republic, and the Position of the South in the Union," 186. Although the biblical meme was commonplace, Cartwright's etymology was apparently novel. Cartwright was unusual in deploying scientific racism in support of slavery. Due to strong antislavery feeling in the scientific community, O'Brien argues, "to jump from race to slavery meant embattlement" (*Conjectures of Order*, 247).

62. Jefferson, *Notes on the State of Virginia*, 170.

63. Ulrich B. Phillips, *Life and Labor in the Old South* (1929; repr., Boston: Little, Brown, 1963), 3, 5.

64. Nathaniel Beverley Tucker, "An Essay of the Moral and Political Effects of the Relation between the Caucasian Master and the African Slave," *Southern Literary Messenger* 10, no. 6 (1844): 330, 333, 334.

65. Kennedy, *Swallow Barn*, 28.

66. Viator, "The Night Funeral of a Slave," *De Bow's Review*

20 (February 1856): 221, 219, 218, 219. Interestingly, the piece had been published and widely reprinted in 1849, occasioning a poem of the same title by Robert H. Thompson. That *De Bow's* reprinted it seven years later suggests its perceived rhetorical power.

67. Anthony Szczesiul, *The Southern Hospitality Myth: Ethics, Politics, Race, and American Memory* (Athens: University of Georgia Press, 2017), 42.

68. C. K. W., "Night Funeral of a Slave," *Liberator*, May 25, 1849, 1.

69. Julius, "Northern and Southern Hospitality," *Philadelphia Repository and Religious and Literary Review* 1, no. 7 (1840): 50.

70. "Historical and Statistical Collections of Louisiana: The Parish of Tensas," *De Bow's Southern and Western Review* 14, no. 5 (1853): 435. For an account of the contentious and labor-intensive nature of the plantation household, see Catherine Clinton, *The Plantation Mistress* (New York: Pantheon, 1982). For an examination of how clock time and rationalist labor practices were integrated into the practice of slavery, see Mark Smith, *Mastered by the Clock: Time, Slavery, and Freedom in the American South* (Chapel Hill: University of North Carolina Press, 1997).

71. "New Links of Union," *Daily Dispatch* (Richmond, Va.), July 28, 1859, 2.

72. T. Pollock Burgwyn, "Farming in North Carolina," *American Farmer* 5, no. 1 (1849): 24.

73. "Miss Fredrika Bremer," *Richmond (Va.) Daily Dispatch*, October 8, 1853, 2.

74. Hundley, *Social Relations in Our Southern States*, 216. In an unusual but significant move, Hundley attributes hospitality to yeoman as well as planter (at least "in a primitive way").

75. Joseph M. Field, "A Lyncher's Own Story," in *Old Southwest Humor from the St. Louis Reveille, 1844–1850*, ed. Fritz Oehlschlaeger (Columbia: University of Missouri Press, 1990), 228.

76. Caroline Lee Hentz, *The Planter's Northern Bride*, vol. 2 (Philadelphia: A. Hart, 1854), 198.

77. John B. Floyd, "Message," in *Governor's Message and Annual Reports* (Richmond: William F. Ritchie, 1849), 16.

78. Horace Bushnell, "Barbarism the First Danger," *National American National Preacher* 21, no. 9 (1847), 209.

79. Hundley, *Social Relations in Our Southern States*, 23–24, 26.

80. "Glimpses at the 'Sunny South,'" *Delaware (Ohio) Gazette*, December 12, 1862, 1.

81. Cecilia, "Memories of Home Travels," *Southern Literary Messenger* 20, no. 3 (1854): 141.

82. John R. Thompson, "Editor's Table," *Southern Literary Messenger* 19, no. 3 (1853): 185, 186.

83. Jacob Abbott, *New England and Her Institutions* (Hartford, Conn.: S. Andrus and Son, 1847), 221, 222, 223.

84. Abbott, *New England and Her Institutions*, 223.

85. "A Day at Summerville," *Southern Literary Journal* 1, no. 3 (1837): 229.

86. John L. McGee, *Southern Chivalry: Arguments versus Club's* (Philadelphia: n.p.: 1856).

87. *Southern Chivalry: The Adventures of G. Whillikens, C.S.A.* (Philadelphia: n.p., 1861), 5.

88. "Song of the Pardon Seekers," *True Southerner*, February 15, 1866, 1. That this journal's name was *True Southerner* is unusual for the time, as prior to the twentieth century, Black people rarely laid claim to the title of southerner.

89. *Weekly North Carolina Standard* (Raleigh), November 13, 1850, 1.

90. Iveson L. Brookes, *A Defence of the South against the Reproaches and Incroachments of the North, in Which Slavery is Shown to be an Institution God Intended to Form the Basis of the Best Social State and the Only Safeguard to the Permanence of Republican Government* (Hamburg, S.C.: n.p., 1850), 32.

91. Brookes, *A Defence of the South against the Reproaches and Incroachments of the North*, n.p.

92. William C. Rives, *History of the Life and Times of James Madison*, vol. 1 (Boston: Little, Brown, 1859), 87–88.

93. John William Draper, *Thoughts on the Future Civil Policy of America* (New York: Harper and Brothers, 1865), 54.

94. Jennifer Rae Greeson, *Our South: Geographic Fantasy and the Rise of National Literature* (Cambridge, Mass.: Harvard University Press, 2010), 186.

95. Harriet Beecher Stowe, *Uncle Tom's Cabin: Or, Life among the Lowly* (Boston: John P. Jewett, 1852), 10.

96. "Mr. Hepworth Dixon on Maryland and Marylanders," *New Eclectic* 2, no. 3 (1868): 354.

97. George Fitzhugh, *Cannibals, All! Or, Slaves without Masters* (Richmond, Va.: A. Morris, 1857), 332, xviii.

98. George Fitzhugh, *Sociology for the South: Or, the Failure of Free Society* (Richmond, Va.: A. Morris, 1854), 27–28, 29, 302.

99. Fitzhugh, *Cannibals, All!*, 334.

100. Calhoun quoted in *Register of Debates in Congress, 24th Congress, 2nd Session* (Washington, D.C.: Gales and Seaton), 719.

101. *Gov. Hammond's Letters on Southern Slavery: Addressed to Thomas Clarkson, the English Abolitionist* (Charleston: n.p., 1845), 3.

102. Edward A. Pollard, *Black Diamonds Gathered in the Darkey Homes of the South* (New York: Pudney and Russell, 1859), 52, 44, 51.

103. "Speech of Hon. W. W. Boyce of South Carolina," *Camden (S.C.) Weekly Journal*, June 13, 1854, 1.

104. J. Quitman Moore, "Southern Civilization: Or, the Norman in America," *De Bow's Review* 12, n.s., nos. 1–2 (1862): 13.

105. Fred Hobson, *The Southern Writer in the Postmodern World* (Athens: University of Georgia Press, 1992), 3.

106. "The South and Her Remedies," *De Bow's Southern and Western Review*, 2, 3rd ser., no. 1 (1851): 7.

107. Floyd, "Message," 19. According to Floyd, "Fanaticism is erecting at our hearth-stones an altar, upon which the victims of sacrifice are to be our wives and daughters." As I argue in the next chapter, southerners eventually began claiming that the hearthstone (or fireside) is what they were defending in a war that seemed to them in retrospect to have little to do with slavery.

108. Yancey quoted in John Witherspoon Du Bose, *The Life and Times of William Lowndes Yancey*, vol. 1 (Birmingham: Roberts and Son, 1892), 301.

109. See Ritchie Devon Watson Jr., *Normans and Saxons: Southern Race Mythology and the Intellectual History of the American Civil War* (Baton Rouge: Louisiana State University Press, 2008), 17–18.

110. Fitzhugh, *Sociology for the South*, 197–98, 29.

111. [George Fitzhugh], "The Message, the Constitution, and the Times," *De Bow's Review* 5, n.s., no. 2 (1861), 162.

112. Moore, *Southern Civilization*, 12.

113. "The Position and Course of the South," *De Bow's Southern and Western Review* 2, 3rd ser., no. 2 (1851): 231–32.

114. "The Basis of Northern Hostility to the South," *De Bow's Review* 3, n.s., no. 1 (1860): 7, 11, 8, 9, 10, 11.

115. O'Brien, *Conjectures of Order*, 250.

116. O'Brien, *Conjectures of Order*, 287.

117. [William Falconer], "The Difference of Race between the Northern and Southern People," *Southern Literary Messenger* 30, no. 6 (1860): 404, 402, 403.

118. Weston, *The Poor Whites of the South* (Washington, D.C.: Buell and Blanchard, 1856), 1.

119. Hinton Rowan Helper, *The Impending Crisis of the South* (New York: Burdick Brothers, 1859), 164, 298.

120. Helper, *The Impending Crisis of the South*, 24, 27, 184, 43, 42, 43.

121. Helper, *The Impending Crisis of the South*, 28, 49, 56, 59, 77, 85, 91, 95, 158, 232, 251, 258, 273.

122. Helper, *The Impending Crisis of the South*, 53, 41. A later edition adds "chevaliers of the lash."

123. Helper, *The Impending Crisis of the South*, vi.

124. George Washington Cable, "Literature in the Southern States," in *The Negro Question*, ed. Arlin Turner (Garden City: Doubleday Anchor, 1958), 44.

125. Singal, *The War Within*, 20.

126. Lewis P. Simpson, *The Dispossessed Garden* (Athens: University of Georgia Press, 1975), 36.

127. Barthes, "Myth Today," 132.

128. Helper, *The Impending Crisis of the South*, 381–82.

129. In *History of the Plots and Crimes of the Great Conspiracy to Overthrow Liberty in America* (1866), John Smith Dye accuses the slave power of assassinating presidents Harrison and Taylor and of attempting to assassinate presidents Jackson and Buchanan.

130. Greeson, *Our South*, 130, 131.

131. "The Combination," *Anti-Slavery Bugle* 6, no. 9 (1850): 1.

132. Brookes, *A Defence of the South against the Reproaches and Incroachments of the North*, 32.

133. "Speech of Mr. Underwood, of Kentucky," May 28, 1850, in *Appendix to the Congressional Globe for the First Session, Thirty-First Congress* (Washington, D.C.: John. C. Rives, 1850), 972.

134. Hammond quoted in "Kansas-Lecompton Constitution," in *Congressional Globe, Thirty-Fifth Congress, 1st Session* (Washington, D.C.: John C. Rives, 1858), 961–62.

135. Henry Wilson, *History of the Rise and Fall of the Slave Power*, vol. 2 (Boston: Houghton, Mifflin, 1874), 178.

136. "The Mud-Sill Speech," *Raftsman's Journal* 5, no. 6 (1858): 2.

137. "Mud Sill Men," *Nevada Democrat*, June 2, 1858, 1.

138. Michael E. Woods, "Mudsills vs. Chivalry," *Muster: How the Past Informs the Present* (blog), December 21, 2018, https://www.journalofthecivilwarera.org/2018/12/mudsills-vs -chivalry/.

139. "Greasy Mechanics, Attention," *New York Daily Tribune*, September 8, 1861, 8.

140. Leonard L. Richards, *The Slave Power: The Free North and Southern Domination, 1780–1860* (Baton Rouge: Louisiana State University Press, 2000), 3.

141. Larry Gara, "Slavery and the Slave Power: A Crucial Distinction," in *Abolition and American Politics and Government*, ed. John R. McKivigan (New York: Garland, 1999), 214. Gara quotes an 1859 letter from H. C. Trinne to Lyman Trumbull.

142. Trescot, "South Carolina," 678.

143. Hammond, quoted in Weston, *Poor Whites of the South*, 3.

144. [Falconer], "The Difference of Race between the Northern and Southern People," 406. To be clear, Falconer isn't excluding Black people from the category of "the true normal race" but whites who lack Norman blood.

145. Harriet Beecher Stowe, *A Key to Uncle Tom's Cabin* (London: Sampson, Low, Son, 1853), 447.

146. Frederick Law Olmsted, *The Cotton Kingdom: A Traveller's Observations on Cotton and Slavery in the American Slave States*, vol. 1 (New York: Mason Brothers, 1861), 11.

147. Hundley, *Social Relations in Our Southern States*, 10, 27, 175, 132, 77, 193, 224, vi, v–vi.

148. Hundley, *Social Relations in Our Southern States*, 270, 276.

149. Hundley, *Social Relations in Our Southern States*, 70, 156, 216, 219, 271, 313, 221, 126.

Chapter 2. The South under Reconstruction

1. Edward A. Pollard, *The Lost Cause: A New Southern History of the War of the Confederates* (New York: E. B. Treat, 1866), 750, 50, 750–51, 751, 50, 699, 404, 615.

2. Pollard, *The Lost Cause*, 751.

3. Benjamin H. Hill Jr., *Senator Benjamin H. Hill of Georgia: His Life, Speeches, and Writings* (Atlanta: T. H. P. Bloodworth, 1893), 193, 335, 335, 337, 336, 339, 327. Hill is eulogized in a piece from a Missouri newspaper reprinted in this volume.

4. See Scott Romine, "Identity as Debate: The Subintellectual History of Edward A. Pollard's *True Southerners*," in *Insiders and Outsiders: Toward a New History of Southern Thought*, ed. Sarah E. Gardner and Steven M. Stowe (Chapel Hill: University of North Carolina Press, 2021), 161–81.

5. Edward A. Pollard, *The Virginia Tourist: Sketches of the Springs and Mountains of Virginia* (Philadelphia: J. B. Lippincott and Co., 1870), 29, 18.

6. Edward A. Pollard, *The Lost Cause Regained* (New York: G. W. Carleton, 1868), 210, 135, 14, 166, 14.

7. Edward A. Pollard, "The Negro in the South," *Lippincott's Magazine of Literature, Science, and Education* 5 (April 1870): 387, 384, 383, 392.

8. See Nancy K. MacLean, *Behind the Mask of Chivalry: The Making of the Second Ku Klux Klan* (New York: Oxford University Press, 1994).

9. J. W. De Forest, "Chivalrous and Semi-Chivalrous Southrons," pt. 1, *Harper's New Monthly Magazine* 38, no. 224 (1869), 192, 193, 192.

10. J. W. De Forrest [*sic*], "Chivalrous and Semi-Chivalrous Southron ," pt. 2, *Harper's New Monthly Magazine* 38, no. 225 (1869): 346, 347.

11. Albert Taylor Bledsoe, "Chivalrous Southrons," *Southern Review* 6, no. 11(1869): 97, 97, 100, 101, 121, 116, 98.

12. Pollard, *The Lost Cause*, 48.

13. Pollard, *The Lost Cause*, 47, 44.

14. Pollard, *The Lost Cause Regained*, 14.

15. Alexander H. Stephens, *A Constitutional View of the Late War between the States*, vol. 1 (Philadelphia: National Publishing Company, 1868), 539.

16. National Park Service, Appomattox Court House National Historical Park, "Why Southern Soldiers Fought," https://www.nps.gov/apco/planyourvisit/upload/Why-Confederates-Fought-Final.pdf. In addition to fighting for "home and family," Confederate soldiers claimed to have fought also for "liberty," "slavery," "honor and duty," and "the draft."

17. W. J. Cash, *The Mind of the South* (1941; repr., New York: Vintage, 1969),, 130.

18. Cash, *The Mind of the South*, 106.

19. Thomas Dixon Jr., *The Leopard's Spots: A Romance of the White Man's Burden, 1865–1900* (New York: Doubleday, Page, 1902), 4.

20. Dominick LaCapra, *History in Transit: Experience, Identity, Critical Theory* (Ithaca, N.Y.: Cornell University Press, 2004), 57.

21. Robert Penn Warren, *The Legacy of the Civil War* (1961; repr., Lincoln: University of Nebraska Press, 1998), 54.

22. William Faulkner, *Intruders in the Dust* (New York: Random House, 1948), 194.

23. Jon Smith, *Finding Purple America: The South and the Future of American Cultural Studies* (Athens: University of Georgia Press, 2013), 35.

24. Dixon, *The Leopard's Spots*, 435. The sole "martyr" of Dixon's novel is Abraham Lincoln, cited, as he often was, as a friend to the South who, had he lived, would have prevented the depredations of Reconstruction (35, 136). Dixon's southern villains are usually former secessionists who convert to the Republican party.

25. Henry Woodfin Grady, "The New South," in *The New South: Writings and Speeches of Henry Grady* (New York: Charles E. Merrill, 1904), 39, 30, 31.

26. Grady, "The New South," 39–40, 30, 31, 27, 37.

27. Grady, "The South and Her Problems," in *The New South*, 85.

28. Henry Watterson, "The New South," in *A Library of American Literature*, vol. 10, ed. Edmund Clarence Stedman and Ellen MacKay Hutchinson (New York: Charles L. Webster, 1891), 54.

29. Dixon, *The Leopard's Spots*, 441, 435.

30. Allen Tate, "Some Remarks on the Southern Religion," in *I'll Take My Stand: The South and the Agrarian Tradition*, by Twelve Southerners (1930; repr., Baton Rouge: Louisiana State University Press, 1977), 169.

31. Cash, *The Mind of the South*, viii.

32. Slavoj Žižek, "Melancholy and the Act," *Critical Inquiry* 26, no. 4 (2000): 658.

33. Richard Gray, *Writing the South: Ideas of an American Region* (1986; repr., Baton Rouge: Louisiana State University Press, 1997), 77.

34. Allen Tate, "A Southern Mode of the Imagination," in *Allen Tate: Essays of Four Decades* (Chicago: Swallow Press, 1968), 586.

35. Letter published in the *Staunton (Va.) Vindicator*, September 3, 1869. The *Vindicator* endorsed the sentiments of a Democratic newspaper in Pennsylvania: "Better take Gen. Lee's advise [*sic*] and let the darned thing die out of remembrance."

36. Henry Timrod, "Ode, Sung of the Occasion of Decorating the Graves of the Confederate Dead, at Magnolia Cemetery, Charleston, S. C., 1867," in *Poems of Henry Timrod* (Richmond, Va.: B. F. Johnson, 1901), 164.

37. Frederick Douglass, "Bombast," *New National Era*, November 10, 1870, 2.

38. "General Lee," *Philadelphia Evening Telegraph*, October 15, 1870, 1.

39. "Louis Herbert's Restaurant," *Cairo Daily Bulletin*, December 29, 1870, 3.

40. Michael Fellman, *The Making of Robert E. Lee* (Baltimore, Md.: Johns Hopkins University Press, 2000), 304.

41. Cash, *The Mind of the South*, 142.

42. Jubal A. Early, *The Campaigns of Gen. Robert E. Lee* (Baltimore, Md.: John Murphy, 1872), 53, 54, 52–53.

43. Eric L. Santner, "Freud's 'Moses' and the Ethics of Nomotropic Desire," *October* 88 (Spring 1999): 22, 23.

44. Eric L. Santner, *On the Psychotheology of Everyday Life: Reflections on Freud and Rosenzweig* (Chicago: University of Chicago Press, 2001), 50, 49.

45. Early, *The Campaigns of Gen. Robert E. Lee*, 51.

46. Fellman, *The Making of Robert E. Lee*, 303, 305–6.

47. Albion Tourgée, *A Fool's Errand* (New York: Fords, Howard, and Hulbert, 1879), 288–89.

48. Cash, *The Mind of the South*, 108.

49. Dixon, *The Leopard's Spots*, 194.

50. Tourgée, *A Fool's Errand*, 289.

51. Dixon, *The Leopard's Spots*, 153.

52. Pollard, *The Lost Cause Regained*, 14.

53. James S. Pike, *The Prostrate State: South Carolina under Negro Government* (New York: Appleton, 1874), 22.

54. Edward King, *The Great South* (Hartford, Conn.: American Publishing Company, 1875), 457.

55. "Brick" Pomeroy, *Soliloquies of the Bondholder, the*

Poor Farmer, the Soldier's Widow, the Political Preacher, the Poor Mechanic, the Freed Negro, the "Radical" Congressman, the Returned Soldier, the Southerner (New York: Van Evrie, Horton, 1866), 15, 2. The sentiment was common among northern Democrats. In an August 27, 1869, article titled "Radical Balderdash," the *Bellefonte (Pa.) Democratic Watchman* complained that the "Radical party" had "sent armies to free the negroes, and then *dared* to make them the political and social peers of the White Race." The *Watchman* insisted that "the people" of the "conquered South," of "that down trodden land," are "bone of our bone and flesh of our flesh, and yet our Radical leaders delight to call up remembrances of the bloody strife and do their utmost to perpetuate unkindly feelings" (1).

56. C. Vann Woodward, *The Burden of Southern History* (Baton Rouge: Louisiana State University Press, 1960), 100–101.

57. William Archibald Dunning, *Reconstruction: Political and Economic, 1865–1877* (New York: Harper and Brothers, 1907), xv.

58. [C. Chauncey Burr], "Editor's Table," *Old Guard* 6, no. 10 (1868): 799.

59. William Lloyd Garrison, editorial, *The Independent*, August 13, 1868, 1.

60. Tourgée, *A Fool's Errand*, 158.

61. J. W. De Forest, "The Colored Member," *Galaxy* 13, no. 3 (1872): 294–95, 294.

62. David W. Blight, *Race and Reunion: The Civil War in American Memory* (Cambridge, Mass.: Harvard University Press, 2001), 211–54.

63. Nina Silber, *The Romance of Reunion: Northerners and the South, 1865–1900* (Chapel Hill: University of North Carolina Press, 1993), 6.

64. Joyce Appleby, "Reconciliation and the Northern Novelist, 1865–1880," *Civil War History* 10, no. 2 (1964): 120.

65. J. W. De Forest, *The Bloody Chasm* (New York: Appleton, 1881), 236.

66. [Stephen T. Robinson], *The Shadow of the War: A Story of the South in Reconstruction Times* (Chicago: Jansen, McClurg, 1884), 6, 8, 35, 11, 157–58, 256.

67. Woodward, *The Burden of Southern History*, 101.

68. Thomas Nast, "Colored Rule in a Reconstructed State," *Harper's Weekly*, March 14, 1874, 229.

69. Thomas Nast, "The Lost Cause: Worse than Slavery," *Harper's Weekly*, October 24, 1874, 878.

70. "Southern Murders," *Philadelphia Evening Telegraph*, October 14, 1868, 2.

71. *Staunton (Va.) Vindicator*, September 3, 1869, 2.

72. Ernest Estercourt, "Letters from the South, by a Northern Hypochondriac," *Southern Magazine* 8, no. 4 (1871): 430, 431, 431, 432.

73. S. H. Canfield, "The Southern Gentleman," *Washington (Ark.) Telegraph*, October 1, 1887, 1.

74. Arkansas, "Powerful Engines," *Washington (Ark.) Telegraph*, October 1, 1887, 1.

75. Mary Adcock, "Southern Heritage," Pinterest, https://www.pinterest.com/pin/263249540689803157/, accessed May 6, 2020.

76. John B. Gordon and Charles C. Jones, *The Old South: Essays Delivered before the Confederate Survivors' Association* (Augusta, Ga.: Chronicle Publishing Company, 1887), 8.

77. Gordon and Jones, *The Old South*, 18, 17.

78. Edwin De Leon, "Ruin and Reconstruction of the Southern States: A Record of Two Tours in 1868 and 1873," pt. 2, *Southern Magazine* 7 (March 1874): 289, 288–89.

79. Gordon and Jones, *Old South*, 17.

80. Grace Elizabeth Hale, *Making Whiteness: The Culture of Segregation in the South, 1890–1940* (New York: Pantheon, 1998), 168–69, 146.

81. Anthony Szczesiul, *The Southern Hospitality Myth: Ethics, Politics, Race, and American Memory* (Athens: University of Georgia Press, 2017), 1–2. Here one is tempted to introduce the term "melancommodity."

82. Albion W. Tourgée, *Bricks without Straw* (New York: Fords, Howard, and Hulbert, 1880), 382, 383.

83. De Leon, "Ruin and Reconstruction of the Southern States," 289.

84. Eugene Genovese, *The Southern Tradition: The Achievement and Limitations of an American Conservatism* (Cambridge, Mass.: Harvard University Press, 1994), 8–9.

85. "The Southern Transformation," *Nation*, November 8, 1866, 370.

86. Edward A. Pollard, *Life of Jefferson Davis* (Philadelphia: National Publishing Company, 1869), 263, 192.

87. "Ring Tournament," *Memphis (Ala.) Public Ledger*, July 14, 1871, 1.

88. Daniel R. Weinfeld, "When We Were Knights: Black Ring Tournaments in the Reconstruction Era," *We're History* (blog), June 5, 2015, https://werehistory.org/black-ring-tournaments/.

89. Lloyd Pratt, "Locality and the Serial South," in *The Oxford Handbook of the Literature of the U.S. South*, ed. Fred Hobson and Barbara Ladd (New York: Oxford University Press, 2016), 104.

90. Arjun Appadurai, *Modernity at Large: Cultural Dimensions of Globalization* (Minneapolis: University of Minnesota Press, 1996), 209.

91. Augustus Baldwin Longstreet, *Augustus Baldwin Longstreet's "Georgia Scenes" Completed*, ed. David Rachels (Athens: University of Georgia Press, 1998), 74.

92. Longstreet quoted in John Donald Wade, *Augustus Baldwin Longstreet: A Study in the Development of Culture in the South* (New York: Macmillan, 1924), 127.

93. Longstreet purchased Augusta's *North American Gazette*, a federalist paper, and renamed it the *State Rights Sentinel* specifically to advocate for state rights following the election of Unionist governor Wilson Lumpkin in 1833.

94. George Washington Cable, "Literature in the Southern States," in *The Negro Question: A Selection of Writings on Civil Rights in the South*, ed. Arlin Turner (New York: Doubleday, 1958), 43–44.

95. John Pendleton Kennedy, *Swallow Barn; or, A Sojourn in the Old Dominion*, vol. 1 (Philadelphia: Carey and Lea, 1832), 77.

96. Michael O'Brien, *Conjectures of Order: Intellectual Life in the American South, 1810–1860*, vol. 1 (Chapel Hill: University of North Carolina Press, 2004), 960.

97. There is a grain of truth in Grady's quip that the New South was simply the Old South under new management: the prewar South was equally committed to profit and confident of obtaining it, although the Old South, as retroactively curated, had little concern for money. Although I've cited *Swallow Barn* as offering an early version of localism, I should note that it was, as Jennifer Rae Greeson acutely observes, in its own time anomalous and anachronistic within the dominant discourses of slavery (*Our South: Geographic Fantasy and the Rise of National Literature* [Cambridge, Mass.: Harvard University Press, 2010], 133).

98. Hammond quoted in "Kansas-Lecompton Constitution," *Congressional Globe*, Thirty-Fifth Congress, 1st Session (Washington, D.C.: John C. Rives, 1858), 962.

99. Bledsoe, "Chivalrous Southrons," 102.

100. Noel Polk, *Outside the Southern Myth* (Jackson: University Press of Mississippi, 1997), xiii.

101. Ted Ownby, "Three Agrarianisms and the Idea of a South without Poverty," in *Reading Southern Poverty between the Wars, 1918–1939*, ed. Richard Godden and Martin Crawford (Athens: University of Georgia Press, 2006), 1, 6.

102. Tate, "A Southern Mode of the Imagination," 581. It bears repeating that the Agrarian project in which Tate took part similarly celebrated a southern "way of life" that scarcely described, or influenced, the way people in the region actually lived, most notably, perhaps, the Agrarians themselves.

103. Michael O'Brien, *Rethinking the South: Essays in Intellectual History* (Baltimore, Md.: Johns Hopkins University Press, 1988)', 216.

104. King, *The Great South*, 17.

105. Thomas Nelson Page, *In Ole Virginia* (New York: Charles Scribner's Sons, 1887), 1.

106. Žižek, "Melancholy and the Act," 659.

107. Svetlana Boym, *The Future of Nostalgia* (New York: Basic Books, 2001), 12, 13.

108. David Mathews, "Coming to Terms with Another New South," in *The Rising South*, vol. 1, ed. Donald R. Noble and Joab L. Thomas (University: University of Alabama Press, 1976), 102. As a member of the Southern Growth Policies Board, Mathews sought to capitalize on a "variety of Southern traditions," including "hospitality," "loving the land," and "community and home." Noting that "the South may indeed have lost much of its distinctiveness," he points out that, "amazingly, 'Southerners' may have been affected little if any at all by the loss." "Southern youth," he reports, still "feel very Southern," adding that "most surprising of all, black students share this same sense" (104).

109. John William Corrigan and Miller Williams, introduction to *Southern Writing in the Sixties: Fiction* (Baton Rouge: Louisiana State University Press, 1966), x.

110. Charles Reagan Wilson, "Place, Sense of," in *The Encyclopedia of Southern Culture*, ed. Charles Reagan Wilson and Wil-

liam Ferris (Chapel Hill: University of North Carolina Press, 1989), 1137.

111. Robert H. Brinkmeyer Jr., "Marginalization and Mobility: Segregation and the Representation of Southern Poor Whites," in *Reading Southern Poverty between the Wars*, 225.

112. Werner Sollors, "Culture, Southern?" *Appalachian Journal* 17, no. 4 (1990): 409.

113. Charles Reagan Wilson, "Manners," in *The Encyclopedia of Southern Culture*, 636.

114. Roland Barthes, "Myth Today," in *A Barthes Reader*, ed. Susan Sontag (New York: Hill and Wang, 1982), 140.

115. As Brooks observes, the killing of Joe Christmas in Faulkner's *Light in August* is not precisely a lynching. It is committed by a single individual, who then castrates Christmas and says, "Now you'll let white women alone even in hell." For Brooks, Christmas's (ambiguous) race is entirely beside the point; he is merely a "pariah." His analysis in, a chapter entitled "The Community and the Pariah," partially provoked my first book, which explores why the *idea* of community, ostensibly there for the taking, seemed to require such elaborate narrative production and maintenance (*William Faulkner: The Yoknapatawpha Country* [New Haven, Conn.: Yale University Press, 1963], 47–74).

116. Cleanth Brooks, "William Faulkner," in *The History of Southern Literature*, ed. Louis D. Rubin Jr., Blyden Jackson, Rayburn S. Moore, Lewis P. Simpson, and Thomas Daniel Young (Baton Rouge: Louisiana State University Press, 1985), 339.

117. Josiah Royce, *Race Questions, Provincialism, and Other American Problems* (New York: Macmillan, 1908), 16.

118. C. Vann Woodward, *The Strange Career of Jim Crow* (1955; repr., New York: Oxford University Press, 2002); Adolph L. Reed Jr., *The South: Jim Crow and its Afterlives* (London: Verso, 2022), 127–29.

119. William Graham Sumner, *Folkways* (Boston: Ginn, 1907), 77; William Archibald Dunning, "The Undoing of Reconstruction," *Atlantic Monthly* 88 (October 1901): 449.

120. George Washington Cable, "The Freedman's Case in Equity," *Century Magazine* 29 (January 1885): 418

121. Henry W. Grady, "In Plain Black and White," *Century Magazine* 29 (March 1885): 909.

122. Grady, "In Plain Black and White," 909, 911.

123. Hinton Rowan Helper, *Nojoque: A Question for a Continent* (New York: George W. Carleton, 1867), v, vii. More speculatively, John William De Forest pondered the question of racial extinction. Observing that "the higher civilization of the Caucasian is gripping the race in many ways, and bringing it to sharp trial before its time," he wonders whether "the negro . . . would remain a negro . . . [or] rather become a ghost" ("The Man and Brother," pt. 2, *Atlantic Monthly* 22 [October 1868]: 425).

124. J. H. Van Evrie, *White Supremacy and Negro Subordination* (New York: Van Evrie, Horton, 1868), 17 (appendix), vi. Thomas Nelson Baker, the first Black PhD recipient at Yale University, also defended the race instinct, which he maintained governed sexual relations, in attacking race prejudice, which he claimed governed social ones. In an essay titled "Intermarriage," he declares the former "sacred and . . . given by the Creator for a sacred purpose" and argues for detaching "social equality" from any association with sexuality (*The Christian Work and Evangelist*, July 20, 1907, 82).

125. A. A. Gundy, "The Problem of Negro Education," *American Journal of Politics* 1 (September 1892): 306.

126. Gundy, "The Problem of Negro Education," 307. From this disordered world, Gundy recalls the "gran[d] picture" of Stonewall Jackson, "the brave chevalier of the South," teaching "a negro Sunday school at Lexington." The grandeur, of course, depended on a world in which everyone was "in their place" (307).

127. Lucinda MacKethan, *The Dream of Arcady: Place and Time in Southern Literature* (Baton Rouge: Louisiana State University Press, 1980), 3.

128. Kennedy, *Swallow Barn*, 37.

129. Caroline Lee Hentz, *The Planter's Northern Bride*, vol. 2 (Philadelphia: A. Hart, 1854), 17.

130. Referring to familiarity in answer to charges that slavery objectified human beings was more effective than William A. Smith's response to Whewell's assertion, which he declares to be "in flat contradiction to the idea of the absorption of the will, the conscience, and the understanding of one man into the personality of another!" (*Lectures on the Philosophy and Practice of Slavery* [Nashville: Stevenson and Evans, 1856], 147–48; Whewell is quoted on 146).

131. Hentz, *The Planter's Northern Bride*, 139. The absolute fidelity and devotion to white children associated with the postwar

mammy is even more conspicuously absent in John S. Robb's "Letters from a Baby" (*Streaks of Squatter Life, and Far-West Scenes* [Philadelphia: T. B. Peterson, 1858]). In the sketch, a white baby complains about his drunken Black nurse and concludes that "the introduction of negro nurses among white babies was a *dark* era in infantile history" (176).

132. Longstreet, "The 'Charming Creature' as a Wife," in *Augustus Baldwin Longstreet's "Georgia Scenes" Completed*, 70.

133. Francis James Robinson, *Kups of Kauphy: A Georgia Book* (Athens, Ga.: Christy and Chelsea, 1853), 86.

134. William Gilmore Simms, *Woodcraft: Or, Hawks about the Dovecoat* (1852; repr., New York: Redfield, 1854), 509.

135. In a comparison of the literary "conception" of the plantation "with the actual," Francis Pendleton Gaines concludes that the two mostly aligned, with the exception of the "altar of devotion" at which the literary (but not actual) slave "sought opportunities for self-immolation." "Dominant in [actual] slave life," he observes, was instead "a mood of forbearance, of patient acceptance, of even rough affection." However, he maintains that the literary tradition of the slave's "self-renunciation" dates to the early nineteenth century, contrary to what I'm claiming (*The Southern Plantation: A Study in the Development and Accuracy of a Tradition* [New York: Columbia University Press, 1924], 227). Certainly there are instances—such as Old Jacques in Caroline Gilman's *Recollections of a Southern Matron* (1838)—but I find them relatively scarce. Quantitative analysis of the question would be helpful.

136. James Lane Allen, "Two Kentucky Gentleman of the Old School," *Century Magazine* 35 (April 1888): 947.

137. Thomas Nelson Page, "Marse Phil," *Century Magazine* 35 (April 1888): 896. The poem combines names and incidents from two of Page's best-known stories, "Marse Chan" and "Meh Lady."

138. Thomas Nelson Page, "Social Life before the War," in *The Old South: Essays Social and Political* (New York: Scribner's, 1906), 166.

139. John Fox Jr., introduction to *The Blue Grass Cook Book*, by Minnie C. Fox (New York: Fox, Duffield, 1904), xii–ix.

140. Cheryl Thurber, "The Development of the Mammy Image and Mythology," in *Southern Women: Histories and Identities*, ed. Virginia Bernhard, Betty Brandon, Elizabeth Fox-Genovese, and Theda Perdue (Columbia: University of Missouri Press, 1992), 96.

141. "Black Mammy Memorial," *Savannah Tribune*, September 23, 1911, 8.

142. William Lightfoot Visscher, *Black Mammy: A Song of the Sunny South, and other Poems* (Cheyenne, Wyo.: Bristol and Knabe, 1886), 14–15.

143. M. M. Manring, *Slave in a Box: The Strange Career of Aunt Jemima* (Charlottesville: University Press of Virginia, 1998), 155–75.

144. Cash, *The Mind of the South*, 131.

145. Jeremy Wells, *Romances of the White Man's Burden: Race, Empire, and the Plantation in American Literature, 1880–1936* (Nashville, Tenn.: Vanderbilt University Press, 2011), 52.

146. Grady, "In Plain Black and White," 914.

147. Cash, *The Mind of the South*, 131.

148. Barthes, "Myth Today," 115. To "love" the myth/meme is, in Barthes words, to consume it "according to the very ends built into its structure"—that is, through the dynamic interaction between referential image and "nebulous condensation."

149. Gundy, "The Problem of Negro Education," 297, 298.

150. Charles W. Kent, preface to *Library of Southern Literature*, vol. 1 (Atlanta: Martin and Holt, 1907), xvi.

151. Anna Julia Cooper, *A Voice from the South, by a Black Woman of the South* (Xenia, Ohio: Aldine, 1892), 100, 217, 101, 108.

152. W. E. B. Du Bois, *The Souls of Black Folk* (Chicago: A. J. McClurg, 1903), 56, 32, 56, 57. Although Du Bois's attitude toward the paternalistic Page and the demagogic Tillman are legible, his view of Aycock is not. While Aycock supported Black education to a degree, his association with the Wilmington massacre and Black disfranchisement were well known by 1903.

153. Ida B. Wells, *The Red Record: Tabulated Statistics and Alleged Causes of Lynching in the United States* (1895; repr., Cavalier Classics, 2015), 90, 13, 90, 83.

154. Booker T. Washington, *Up from Slavery: An Autobiography* (New York: Doubleday, 1901), 194, 246.

155. Michael O'Brien, *Placing the South* (Jackson: University Press of Mississippi, 2007), 132.

156. Stanley Elkins, *Slavery: A Problem in American Institutional and Intellectual Life* (1959; repr., New York: Grosset and Dunlap, 1963), 86.

157. Trudier Harris, *From Mammies to Militants: Domestics in Black American Literature* (Philadelphia: Temple University Press, 1973), 37.

158. Jefferson Humphries, "The Discourse of Southernness: Or How We Can Know There Will Still Be Such a Thing as the South and Southern Literary Culture in the Twenty-First Century," in *The Future of Southern Letters*, ed. Jefferson Humphries and John Lowe (New York: Oxford University Press, 1996), 120, 131.

159. "The Cook Whose Cabin Became More Famous than Uncle Tom's," advertisement, *Ladies' Home Journal* 36 (October 1919): 153; "When Guests Dropped in to Stay a Week or Two," advertisement, *Ladies' Home Journal* 36 (November 1919): 116.

160. "How Aunt Jemima Saved the Colonel's Mustache and His Reputation as Host," advertisement, *Ladies' Home Journal* 37 (October 1920): 173; "Gray Morn," advertisement, *Saturday Evening Post*, November 20, 1920, 112; "When the *Rob't E. Lee* Stopped at Aunt Jemima's Cabin," advertisement, *Saturday Evening Post*, December 18, 1920, 40.

161. "At the World's Fair in '93 Aunt Jemima Was a Sensation," advertisement, *Ladies' Home Journal* 38 (March 1921): 86.

162. Karen L. Cox, *Dreaming of Dixie: How the South Was Created in American Popular Culture* (Chapel Hill: University of North Carolina Press, 2011), 4, 5.

163. Raymond Egan and Richard A. Whiting, *They Made It Twice as Nice as Paradise: And They Called it Dixieland* (New York: Jerome H. Redick, 1916).

164. T. Harry Williams, *Romance and Realism in Southern Politics* (Athens: University of Georgia Press, 1961), 7.

165. Donald Davidson, "Gulliver with Hay Fever," *American Review* 9, no. 2 (1937): 152, 152, 154, 153, 153–54.

166. Tate quoted in R. H. Mitchell, "Images of Virginia: Allen Tate, the Agrarians, and the Old South" (MA thesis, College of William and Mary, 1979), 7.

Chapter 3. The South Is a Bad Idea

1. Anthony Lewis, "Segregation Group Confers in Secret," *New York Times*, December 30, 1955, 12.

2. George C. Wallace, inaugural address, Alabama Department of Archives and History, 2, https://digital.archives.alabama.gov /digital/collection/voices/id/2952/, accessed June 16, 2022.

3. "Declaration of Constitutional Principles," *Congressional Record*, March 12, 1956, 4460.

4. Americans overall responded similarly, with 56 percent reporting they saw the flag as racist and 35 percent that they regarded it as signifying pride for the South. See Nicholas Reimann, "Majority of Southerners Now View the Confederate Flag as a Racist Symbol," *Forbes*, July 15, 2020, https://www.forbes.com/sites/nicholasreimann/2020/07/15/majority-of-southerners-now-view-the-confederate-flag-as-a-racist-symbol-poll-finds/?sh=3f8f2d162c7a.

5. W. J. Cash, *The Mind of the South* (1941; repr., New York: Vintage, 1969), vii.

6. John Shelton Reed, *My Tears Spoiled My Aim: Reflections on Southern Culture* (Columbia: University of Missouri Press, 1993), 22–27; Christopher A. Cooper and H. Gibbs Knotts, "Declining Dixie: Regional Identification in the Modern American South," *Social Forces* 88, no. 3 (March 2010): 1083–1101.

7. Nicole Mumphrey, "Dixie Beer Enlisting the Public's Help in Its Renaming Efforts," Fox8Live, September 21, 2021, https://www.fox8live.com/2020/09/21/dixie-beer-enlisting-publics-help-its-renaming-efforts/.

8. Susan Knox, "Lady Antebellum Apologise as They Change Name amid Black Lives Matter Movement," *Mirror*, June 11, 2020, https://www.mirror.co.uk/3am/celebrity-news/lady-antebellum-apologise-change-name-22177704.

9. "Why We Created the *Bitter Southerner* in the First Place," *Bitter Southerner*, August 6, 2013, https://bittersoutherner.com/we-are-bitter. For the T-shirt, see *Bitter Southerner*, https://bsgeneralstore.com/products/the-tomato-sandwich-t-shirt, accessed June 1, 2021.

10. Melissa Locker, "Southern Traditions We Want to Bring Back—And You Will Too," *Southern Living*, November 3, 2022, https://www.southernliving.com/culture/southern-manners-customs-traditions.

11. Cash, *The Mind of the South*, viii.

12. Cash, *The Mind of the South*, viii; Ulrich B. Phillips, "The Central Theme of Southern History," *American Historical Review*, 34, no. 1 (928): 31.

13. Allen Tate to Lincoln Kirsten, May 10, 1933, quoted in Mark Malvasi, *The Unregenerate South* (Baton Rouge: Louisiana State University Press, 1997), 208.

14. Malvasi, *The Unregenerate South*, 208.

15. Allen Tate to Donald Davidson, October 19, 1962, quoted in Malvasi, *The Unregenerate South*, 208.

16. Eugene Genovese, *The Southern Tradition: The Achievement and Limitations of an American Conservatism* (Cambridge, Mass.: Harvard University Press, 1994), 88.

17. Fred Hobson, *The Southern Writer in the Postmodern World* (Athens: University of Georgia Press, 1992), 101.

18. Christopher A. Cooper and H. Gibbs Knotts, *The Resilience of Southern Identity* (Chapel Hill: University of North Carolina Press, 2017), 13, 23.

19. Charles Reagan Wilson, "Place, Sense of," in *The Encyclopedia of Southern Culture*, ed. Charles Reagan Wilson and William Ferris (Chapel Hill: University of North Carolina Press, 1989), 1138.

20. John Shelton Reed, *The Enduring South: Subcultural Persistence in Mass Society* (1972; Chapel Hill: University of North Carolina Press, 1986), 36, 36–37.

21. Jon Smith, "Big Two-Hearted Essay," 5, Academia.edu, https://www.academia.edu/25346313/Big_Two_Hearted_Essay, accessed March 31, 2023.

22. When I ask my students to consider how many of their experiences of the past twenty-four hours of their lives—the things they've done, the media they've consumed, the places they've gone, the food they've eaten, their interactions with others, and so forth—could be plausibly described as representative of "the southern way of life," the answer is generally not many of them.

23. Brad Watson, "On Southern Literature and a Sense of Place," *Book Riot*, August 10, 2016, https://bookriot.com/on-southern-literature-and-a-sense-of-place/.

24. Kwame Anthony Appiah, *The Lies That Bind: Rethinking Identity* (New York: Liveright, 2018), 199.

25. C. Hugh Holman, *Three Modes of Southern Fiction: Ellen Glasgow, William Faulkner, Thomas Wolfe* (1966; repr., Athens: University of Georgia Press, 2008), xiii.

26. Richard Gray, "Inventing Communities, Imagining Places," in *South to a New Place*, ed. Suzanne W. Jones and Sharon Monteith (Baton Rouge: Louisiana State University Press, 2002), xxiii. Interestingly, Gray begins with a dialogic, oppositional account of southern identity and readily concedes that the South "has never not been made up of a number of castes, classes, and smaller com-

munities" standing in uneasy relation or active conflict with those who claim that *"their* South is *the* South" (xviii).

27. Wendell Berry, "The Regional Motive," in *A Continuous Harmony: Essays Cultural and Agriculture* (New York: Harcourt Brace Jovanovich, 1972), 64, 67.

28. For the "South without Borders" T-shirt, see *Bitter Southerner*, https://web.archive.org/web/20190406233041/https://bsgeneralstore .com/products/south-without-border-t-shirt, accessed via Internet Archive Wayback Machine, August 7, 2023.

29. Margaret T. McGehee, "The Online Merch-ing of Whiteness," in *Remediating Region: New Media and the U.S. South*, ed. Gina Caison, Stephanie Rountree, and Lisa Hinrichsen (Baton Rouge: Louisiana State University Press, 2021), 115.

30. Michael O'Brien, *Rethinking the South: Essays in Intellectual History* (Baltimore, Md.: Johns Hopkins University Press, 1988), 236, 235.

31. Tracy Thompson, "Dixie Is Dead," *Bitter Southerner*, https://bittersoutherner.com/dixie-is-dead-tracy-thompson -defining-the-south.

32. In his 1882 "What Is a Nation?," Renan claims that "the act of forgetting, I would even say, historical error, is an essential factor in the creation of a nation, which is why progress in historical studies often constitutes a danger for nationality. Indeed, historical enquiry brings back to light the deeds of violence that took place at the origin of all political formations, even those whose consequences have been the most beneficial" (*What Is a Nation? And Other Political Writings*, ed. and trans. M. F. N. Giglioli [New York: Columbia University Press, 2018], 251).

33. Scott Romine, "God and the Moon Pie: Consumption, Disenchantment, and the Reliably Lost Cause," in *Creating and Consuming the U.S. South*, ed. Martyn Bone, Brian Ward, and William A. Link (Gainesville: University Press of Florida, 2015), 49–71.

34. Lewis Grizzard, "The Story of 'True Grits,'" *Atlanta (Ga.) Journal-Constitution*, November 10, 2019, X3.

35. Seth Stephens-Davidowitz, *Everybody Lies: Big Data, New Data, and What the Internet Can Tell Us about Who We Really Are* (New York: HarperCollins, 2017), 7.

36. Imani Perry, *South to America: A Journey below the Mason-Dixon to Understand the Soul of a Nation* (New York: HarperCollins, 2022), 14.

37. Marcus Anthony Hunter and Zandria F. Robinson, *Chocolate Cities: The Black Map of American Life* (Oakland: University of California Press, 2018), 2, 3. Their argument regarding the manufactured distinction between North and South, in turn, restates the argument of Matthew Lassiter and Joseph Crespino in *The Myth of Southern Exceptionalism* (Oxford: Oxford University Press, 2008).

38. Stephen Menedian, Samir Gambhir, and Arthur Gailes, "The Roots of Structural Racism Project: Twenty-First Century Racial Residential Segregation in the United States." Othering and Belonging Institute, June 21, 2021, https://belonging.berkeley.edu/roots-structural-racism.

39. Hunter and Robinson, *Chocolate Cities*, 4.

40. Charles Love, "I Spent the Summer in the South: What They're Telling You about Racism There Is Wrong," *Newsweek*, September 13, 2021, https://www.newsweek.com/i-spent-summer-south-what-theyre-telling-you-about-racism-there-wrong-opinion-1628545.

41. Jemar Tisby, "I'm a Black Man Who Moved to the Deep South: Here's What It's Teaching Me about Race," *Vox*, January 4, 2019, https://www.vox.com/first-person/2017/10/31/16571238/black-man-deep-south-race.

42. Connor quoted in William Nunnelley, *Bull Connor* (Tuscaloosa: University of Alabama Press, 1991), 154; Romaine Smith, "The South Is Football Country," *Southern Living* 1, no. 8 (1966): 53.

43. Gina Caison, Stephanie Rountree, and Lisa Hinrichsen, introduction to *Remediating Region*, 3.

44. Eugene Butler, "Southern Living: In Tune with Today's South," *Southern Living* 1, no. 1 (1966): 1.

45. E. L. Holland Jr., "The Bright Modern South That Writers Are Missing," *Southern Living* 1, no. 10 (1966): 70.

46. "City with a Clean Face and Forward Look," *Southern Living* 1, no. 3 (1966): 66, 67.

47. Caison, Rountree, and Hinrichsen, introduction, 3–4.

48. "Atlanta," *Southern Living* 1, no. 4 (1966): 57, 58.

49. Sarah Shields Pfeiffer, "Try Aunt Fanny's Cabin," *Southern Living* 1, no. 6 (1966): 38.

50. Amy J. Elias, "Postmodern Southern Vacation: Vacation Advertising, Globalization, and Southern Regionalism," in *South to a New Place*, 266.

51. Elias, "Postmodern Southern Vacation," 264, 265.

52. And yet how easily we take to the idea that the older way of life was organic and real, an authentic version of what is now simulated, commodified, or otherwise degraded. But as Edward Ayers observes, the declension narrative of a once-rooted and unified South dates to the early nineteenth century ("What We Talk about When We Talk about the South," in *All Over the Map: Rethinking American Regions*, ed. Edward Ayers, Patricia Nelson Limerick, Stephen Nissenbaum, and Peter S. Onuf [Baltimore, Md.: Johns Hopkins University Press, 1996], 69).

53. Alex Haley, foreword to *The Encyclopedia of Southern Culture*, xi.

54. Hunter and Robinson, *Chocolate Cities*, 4.

55. Scott Romine, *The Real South: Southern Narrative in the Age of Cultural Reproduction* (Baton Rouge: Louisiana State University Press, 2008), 236.

56. Benedict Anderson, *Imagined Communities: Reflections on the Origin and Spread of Nationalism* (1983; London: Verso, 2006), 34–48; Niall Ferguson, "Russia's Farcical Mutiny Is Deadly Serious for China and Iran," *Bloomberg*, July 2, 2023, https://www.bloomberg.com/opinion/articles/2023-07-02/russia-s -farcical-mutiny-is-deadly-serious-for-iran-china-niall-ferguson.

57. The persistence of Confederate memes strikes me as an important area of inquiry, although I have little understanding of it. I am particularly unsure of the regionalist implications of the Confederate flag, which seems to function less like the Basque flag does—that is, a symbol of separatist aspiration—than as a symbol of the kind of populist, ethnonationalist movements that have arisen in many liberal democracies. Thus (unlike the Basque flag) it is more likely to appear alongside the American flag than to be "flown against it" and to be borrowed by "rural Canadian weirdos" (Brad Casey, "Why Are Dumb Canadians Waving the Confederate Flag?" *Vice*, March 7, 2013, https://www.vice.com/en/article /5gqw7n/why-are-dumb-canadians-waving-the-confederate-flag).

58. Anthony Szczesiul, *The Southern Hospitality Myth: Ethics, Politics, Race, and American Memory* (Athens: University of Georgia Press, 2017), 210.

59. Locker, "Southern Traditions We Want to Bring Back."

60. "At the World's Fair in '93 Aunt Jemima Was a Sensation," advertisement, *The Ladies' Home Journal* 38 (March 1921): 86.

61. M. M. Manring, *Slave in a Box: The Strange Career of Aunt Jemima* (Charlottesville: University Press of Virginia, 1998), 177.

62. This text originally appeared on the Sweet Home Alabama website but has been removed (http://www.alabama.travel /experience-alabama/hospitality). As Szczesiul observes, the webpage coincided with the imposition of strict anti-immigration legislation in Alabama, although the ensuing conversation in Alabama over the ethical imperatives of hospitality offered hopeful signs that the principle might be "oriented toward the future and the arrival of new strangers" (*The Southern Hospitality Myth*, 213-218).

63. McGehee, "The Online Merch-ing of Whiteness," 115, 116.

64. Amber Sutton, "How to Make the Perfect Tomato Sandwich," *Alabama Life and Culture*, June 29, 2022, https://www .al.com/life/2022/06/how-to-make-the-perfect-tomato-sandwich .html; "Diet of the Teetotaler," *Alexandria Gazette*, October 21, 1911, 6.

65. Statista reports that in 2016, Miracle Whip accounted for 13.6 percent of sales in the eastern United States, while Duke's accounted for 7.5 percent; the figures for the central United States were 28.6 percent and 4.1 percent, respectively. See "United States: Brand Preferences for Mayonnaise in 2016, by Region," Statista, https://www.statista.com/statistics/623858 /us-brand-preferences-for-mayonnaise-region/.

66. Eva Greene Fuller, *The Up-to-Date Sandwich Book: 400 Ways to Make a Sandwich* (Chicago: A. C. McClurg, 1909), 41.

67. "Domestic Concerns," *River Falls (Wis.) Journal*, September 10, 1891, 1.

68. Kim Alexander, Phillip Rhodes, and Caroline Sanders, "*G&G*'s Great Mayonnaise Taste Test," *Garden and Gun*, March 14, 2019, https://gardenandgun.com/articles/ggs-great-mayonnaise -taste-test/.

69. Southern Fried Cotton, https://southernfriedcotton.com.

70. Shane Mitchell, "A Hunger for Tomatoes," *Bitter Southerner*, September 25, 2018, https://bittersoutherner.com/a-hunger -for-tomatoes-shane-mitchell. As is often the case with *Bitter Southerner*, the "our" here—the southerners who possess the hunger for tomatoes and *ought* to be concerned about unfair labor practices is implicitly different from "the people in the fields."

71. George Washington Cable, *John March, Southerner* (New York: Charles Scribner's Sons, 1894), 326.

72. For the T-shirt, see https://bsgeneralstore.com/products /the-bitter-southerner-beliefs-shirt, accessed September 29, 2020.

73. Efforts to, as Barthes says, "immuniz[e] the contents of the collective imagination by means of a small inoculation of ac- knowledged evil" can assemble different groups ("Myth Today," in *A Barthes Reader*, ed. Susan Sontag [New York: Hill and Wang, 1982], 140). *Bitter Southerner* concedes that "it's still too damned easy for folks to draw the conclusion that we Southern- ers are hopelessly bound to tradition" and advises that if "you still think women look really nice in hoop skirts, we politely sug- gest you find other amusements on the web." ("Why We Created the *Bitter Southerner* in the First Place"). D. C. McAllister, how- ever, argues similarly that the South's "racist past" is "part of it, but not all of it," but defends hoop skirts as part of the South's "proud and vibrant heritage" ("Hoop Skirts Mean Freedom, Not Oppression," *Federalist*, September 10, 2015, https://thefederalist .com/2015/09/10/hoop-skirts-mean-freedom-not-oppression/).

74. Eric Gary Anderson, Taylor Hagood, and Daniel Cross Turner, introduction, to *Undead Souths: The Gothic and beyond in Southern Literature and Culture* (Baton Rouge: Louisiana State University Press, 2015), 6.

75. O'Brien, *Rethinking the South*, 217; Michael O'Brien, *Plac- ing the South* (Jackson: University Press of Mississippi, 2007), 19, 114, 19.

76. In retrospect, it seems curious that, to my knowledge, no graduate student of the 1990s ever published an essay entitled "De- constructing the South," in which the "North/South" binary would have been exposed as . . . whatever deconstructionists exposed things as. Similarly, no essay borrowed Judith Butler's conception of gender performativity to suggest that southernness was performa- tive. There were hundreds of iterations of those essays, which sug- gests, perhaps, the South's peculiar resistance to "deconstruction."

77. Bruno Latour, *Reassembling the Social: An Introduction to Actor-Network Theory* (Oxford: Oxford University Press, 2005), 186.

78. As Jon Smith and I argue in *The Strange Career of Corn- bread Nation* (forthcoming), food memes have proven especially effective in evoking an essentialized and romanticized South.

79. Richard Dawkins, *The Extended Selfish Gene* (Oxford: Oxford University Press, 1989), 200.

80. Cooper and Knotts, *The Resilience of Southern Identity*, 22, 23, 25, 6, 12, 16. Regarding the question as to whether Mississippi taxpayers who learned there was such an entity as the Center for the Study of Southern Culture would support it, my guess is that they probably would if they thought it would counter lingering stigmata associated with poverty and backwardness with homages to "Faulkner" and "foodways" but might reconsider if they read the work of scholars associated with it.

81. Cooper and Knotts, *The Resilience of Southern Identity*, 74, 74, 75, 89, 89.

82. Walter Hines Page, *The Southerner* (1909; repr., Columbia: University of South Carolina Press, 2008), 390. In the course of writing an introduction to the novel, I noticed Page's reworking of Du Bois's concept of double consciousness. During a trip to undertake research at Harvard's Houghton Library, I struck up a conversation with a hotel concierge while waiting for a cab. After learning that I had come from North Carolina, he made several confusing (to me) statements, until I finally came to understand that he was trying to put me at ease by conveying that he held no negative stereotypes of southerners. It struck me at the time that this was my first "serious" experience of what Page was describing.

83. Cooper and Knotts, *The Resilience of Southern Identity*, 90, 91, 76, 76, 76, 75–76, 87, 80.

84. O'Brien, *Placing the South*, 114.

85. Cooper and Knotts, *The Resilience of Southern Identity*, 90, 84, 87, 82, 83.

86. Jon Smith, *Finding Purple America: The South and the Future of American Cultural Studies* (Athens: University of Georgia Press, 2013), 49.

87. Manring, *Slave in a Box*, 10.

Index

Selected books from the Mercer University Lamar Memorial Lectures

Remapping Southern Literature:
Contemporary Southern Writers and the West
Robert H. Brinkmeyer Jr.

A Web of Words: The Great Dialogue of Southern Literature
Richard Gray

Remembering Medgar Evers:
Writing the Long Civil Rights Movement
Minrose Gwin

The Power of the Porch: The Storyteller's Craft in
Zora Neale Hurston, Gloria Naylor, and Randall Kenan
Trudier Harris

The Southern Writer in the Postmodern World
Fred Hobson

A Late Encounter with the Civil War
Michael Kreyling

The North of the South: The Natural World and the National Im-
aginary in the Literature of the Upper South
Barbara Ladd

Daughters of Time: Creating Woman's Voice in Southern Story
Lucinda H. MacKethan

Hidden in Plain Sight: Slave Capitalism in
Poe, Hawthorne, and Joel Chandler Harris
John T. Matthews